How to Beat the
Game When Y...

Other Motoring Paperfronts

How to Beat the Second-hand Car Game When You Buy or Sell

by

B. C. Macdonald

(author of the 'Car Doctor A–Z,' 'Car Repairs Properly Explained' and the Paperfront 'Popular Models' series of repair manuals)

and

A. Tom Topper

(author of 'Learning to Drive in Pictures' and 'Very Advanced Driving' Paperfronts)

PAPERFRONTS
ELLIOT RIGHT WAY BOOKS
KINGSWOOD, SURREY, U.K.

Made and printed in Great Britain by
Cox & Wyman Ltd., London, Reading and Fakenham

CONTENTS

LIST OF ILLUSTRATIONS

Please start here

The aim of this book is to clear the 'fog' in which so many people become immersed when they come to buy, or sell, a second hand car. The mystery is spread thick in this game. What with part exchange, 'guarantees', low deposit easy terms and all the rest, it is not surprising that many motor salesmen rub their hands with glee when yet another 'punter' walks through the showroom door.

A person is particularly likely to make his biggest mistake when buying *the* car he always wanted. His personal longing for *that* car is likely to overrule his common sense. After weeks or months of anxious looking, waiting, perhaps even advertising, when *the* car appears within his grasp at last, he suddenly finds he has agreed to a deal which will later be seen to be a 'classic' error of judgement. Perhaps he has misjudged the market value; if a buyer, maybe he forgot a vital mechanical check; if a seller he might find he has sold a valuable accessory for 'nothing'; often a 'close' friend or a family squabble have pushed him against his own better judgement – there are scores of pitfalls for the unwary.

Within an evening or two of light reading we hope to lead the prospective buyer/seller through all these smokescreens and enable him to make a clear, commercially logical decision, without panic, when the time comes to make the deal.

In buying, just as much as in selling, the right psychology is vital. In the old days horse traders deftly employed every known psychological nicety in striking the best bargains for themselves. For hard bargaining none were better! Today car dealers have inherited, and improved this expertise.

But the private buyer or seller who knows the game can give as good as he gets. And if he is dealing with another private individual he can put himself at an advantage by handling things in the right way and avoiding a few common mistakes.

Good luck!

B.C.M.
A.T.T.

1

Checking Market Prices

The market price of any car, that is to say the price at which supply and demand balance, should be the same whether one is a buyer or a seller.

In considering what that price should be, a buyer or seller can easily compare prices of *exactly* similar models. With a little research either should be able to arrive reasonably accurately by the same methods to within a few pounds of a fair market value for a car of the type in question in 'average' condition. On cheaper cars this will certainly be within 8–10 per cent error either way, ranging up to say 15 per cent on the more expensive models.

Compare Like with Like
In arriving at a figure it is vital that comparisons are made only with *exactly* similar models and that one looks in the right media for the type of car. Any variations to specification that were originally offered new by the manufacturers ('optional' extras) need to have due allowance made for them. For example a larger engine, or automatic transmission, or a 'GT' conversion may merit a little more on the price. Not only must the model be the same for true comparison, the year and approximate month of original manufacture and registration have to be the same or very close and the mileage covered should not be markedly different.

Geographical Location
Where the car is will make a difference. Remote areas have a smaller market than big towns; a capital city can usually

11

command higher prices than a far away provincial town. This geographical factor is well worth investigation if an unusual car is being considered, such as a high-priced sports car or anything which is rare. It may pay the seller to adverise far and near to widen his market or a buyer to look in unlikely places, for the most advantageous price.

Extras

Fortunately, from the buyer's point of view, added on accessories count for little – a conversely unfortunate fact for the seller, but all this you will find discussed more fully on page 39. So you can leave 'extras' out of your calculations.

Timing

Seasonal factors are reflected in prices. Although the physical age of the car may only be a month different, if it was first put on the road in December, rather than the following January, it will be a previous year car.

If, as in Great Britain, the number plate proclaims how old the car is by means of a letter or number tacked on, then the more recently coded car fetches a higher price. The number plate differences are rarely substantial except in the first couple of years but you will find a younger coding is emphasized when this is advantageous and glossed over when it is not.

But the calendar year counts for a lot. A January car may easily fetch 10 per cent or more extra compared to an identical sister car put on the road only weeks earlier in the previous December. At the £1,000 level this makes a difference of £100! This is why new car buyers mainly hold off towards the end of the year so that they can register on 2nd January in the new year. The reason for this year end phenomenon seems to be that there has to be *somewhere* for a line to be drawn on prices and that the 31st December has become the mutually convenient point worked to by the majority in the car industry.

A car first registered in December therefore may turn out

to be a much better 'buy' second hand than its January equivalent if the mileage and condition are equal, because of the price advantage.

Re-vamped Models
A face lift to the model by the manufacturer during the production run will knock a few pounds off the earlier models, as people tend to wait till the Mark II, or whatever, percolates through to the second hand market. Much depends on what you personally think of the changes that were made whether you wish to pay any more in order to have them. But you must not lose sight of the fact that it is not what *you* think that necessarily counts. Everyone has a different view and what matters in the end is what the market *in general* desires, no matter whether its reasoning is logical, or fanciful, or can be ascertained, or not!

Day-to-day Watch on Prices
Second hand prices are revised downwards (very occasionally, it's upwards!) every few weeks. In an economic crash it may even be by hundreds of pounds every few days, but you will nearly always notice a change, for the same car, as each month goes by. It is therefore essential to make your assessment in one go, in the ways explained below, and then to keep up to date with the downward (or upward) trend if the months start to slip by before you make a deal. It is worth noting when the next *Glass's Guide* is due out — see page 23.

Condition Compared to the Average
An 'average' 1–2 year old well maintained car should have little or no immediate expensive attention required, although there are always the rogues that ruin the rule. A 2–3 year old well kept car will be likely to need something important but hopefully, nothing too cripplingly expensive. A 4–6 year old car may still look in good shape but be masking a serious fault; however your careful examination should

13

have uncovered it unless you are very unlucky. Older cars are always a gamble. (See page 18 *Spare Parts*.)

Bearing this in mind the particular car to which you are directing your attention can thus be evaluated against the 'average' price which your research has ascertained. Chapter 2 shows what to look for with regard to mechanical condition, and which faults may render a body not worth wasting any further time upon. After examination you will be able to tot up in your mind the cost of repairs which will clearly be necessary and deduct this from what you are prepared to pay. Or you can steel yourself to pay a little over the average for something in good order. A little enquiry at your local garage or panel beater will be sufficient for you to work out how much repairs might be going to cost. Usually, it's more than you think!

Which Media?
Unless you are a car enthusiast, familiar with the motoring press, you will probably need to browse around a good magazine retailer to discover which motoring magazines to buy. Not all carry *much* second hand car advertising. The most up-to-date ones may be the weeklies but it depends how long ago the monthlies came out. Don't forget to ask if any are due out shortly.

What Car? magazine, a Haymarket Publication, is a useful monthly journal which includes an up-to-date guide to the prices of new models and, in addition, it sets out guide lines to prices of second-hand examples of the majority of models, according to age and allowing for an average mileage. The basis upon which the prices are marked is described in the magazine itself. Month by month the magazine staff test various cars and give a thorough going and fair report. Also included in the reference section is a very useful category index which enables the reader to see exactly how wide the choice is of possible cars which would suit his purposes. For instance, in a recent issue, the following examples of categories were included: open sports cars: three and five door saloons: estate cars: economy cars – 40 m.p.g. plus. As mentioned on page 56 it is a great mistake to buy the wrong car for your purposes. Therefore, this magazine is likely to be a great help if you have any doubts. It is worth watching each month to see if a special report on the car in which you are interested comes out.

Daily and Sunday national newspapers are worth study, particularly for luxury expensive models, and you should find a large classified section in your evening paper. At the popular end of the market a lot of cars are advertised in those local and weekly papers that exist largely as a forum for the sale of second hand goods and property.

The best concentration of advertising for an unusual car may be found in a less usual medium. For example a motor racing journal could be the right place to look for some exceptionally fast road car, or, for a Rolls-Royce, it might be the *Financial Times*. Certain media have become the 'Shop window' for out of the ordinary groups such as American cars or motor caravans.

In looking at classified small ads. remember that a large percentage will have been put there by motor traders. Some will be obvious but some are disguised and may be detected as described on page 28.

In all these places you are likely to find a lot of display advertisements by the motor trade. Comb these too, in making your price assessment.

Your local papers carry lots of display ads. by *local* garages. Studying these tells you who nearby deals in the type of car you are concerned with and shows up any differences on prices peculiar to your area.

Wading through pages of advertisements may seem very tiresome but, since they are mainly grouped by type of car it is not so very difficult in practice. Another way to get the feel of the market, which should be used as well, and which can be done by and by in your travels, is to look round used car displays. The only danger is falling in love with the first car you see and buying in haste at the wrong price!

You will observe people of a haggling disposition (mentioned again on page 75) who advertise high prices and expect to be 'beaten down'. You can allow for this. A fairly safe rule, however, is that the prices asked by reputable traders are firm prices. They expect the car will sell for their price and the advertisement does not conceal an intention to drop, even by a fiver.

Supply and Demand

The market price of any car reflects current opinion of its value. Its true worth is what someone *will pay* for it. How many buyers of this model are around? How plentiful is the supply? How long can you wait? All the threads of knowledge which percolate around the market about this or that make of car will have been accounted for in the making of its market price.

By arriving at the correct price for the car you are *buying* or *selling* in the ways described you take advantage of market knowledge and avoid having to worry about the myriad of factors which affect prices.

Economic Climate

Sometimes shrewd judgement of whether to wait a while before buying, or perhaps to sell quickly can save a lot of cash.

In boom conditions luxury cars sell well. In a recession they stick. However the market is very quick to 'discount' the effects of a forthcoming economic decline. This means to say that prices are moved down *ahead* of the crash to allow for the worst *before* it comes. Equally when better times are on the way, car prices tend to be one of the first things to creep upwards. When a crash looms near there is an old saying in the motor trade that 'the first loss is the best one to take'. If a panic begins to run it is sometimes best to be the first to panic!

A few hours can make all the difference. For example one day recently I had a Mini estate car to sell quickly for cash. The company concerned instructed me to take the best offer I could find that very day. With no time to advertise the only way was to call on a reasonable number of dealers and show them the car. The best offer turned out to be the third offer made, before lunchtime. By the time I returned to accept it in the early afternoon the buyer had received a directive from his group managing director to buy nothing more as from 12 o'clock! The market was crashing so fast that they had decided to stand still and wait for price levels to stabilize. If they were right they would soon be able to buy plenty of cars for much less money. Luckily I found an equal offer by the end of the afternoon to the clear relief of the company I was selling the car for. How right their view of the economic climate had been proved!

If new prices are about to go up, second hand prices of low mileage examples of the same model will hold up.

Shortages and Unusually High Demand

If there has been an acute shortage of the car during the early stages of its production run and there is plenty of demand, second hand prices will remain good till supply catches up. End of production of a competing model may make yours worth more.

Whenever a new model is introduced by a manufacturer, unless he has built more production space, you can be sure an older model is about to be phased out. Will it be your model?

The original price of the car when new cannot be taken as any guide to its second hand value. Some new cars have been so hard to obtain that the second hand price after a year has still been higher than it cost new! Generally, however, the higher the initial price the faster it falls. After this depreciation has levelled off such a car may prove an excellent 'buy' for a man who does a small annual mileage and likes some prestige. The higher running costs are more than offset by the low buying price.

When industrial (in) action or whatever puts a lot of *new* cars in short supply you can expect a firm second hand market with good prices being fetched all round. But if showrooms are packed with new cars the second hand market will be correspondingly poor.

Spare Parts

New car sales, at prices which have to show a profit over current production costs, are dependent on buoyant (high) second hand prices. If second hand cars are excessively good value fewer people will be inclined to buy new while this condition lasts. To ensure a strong second hand market manufacturers know that they must continue to provide spare parts availability for at least ten years. New car buyers are easily put off if word gets around that a model will have a poor second hand value. Thus you can be fairly certain that parts will be obtainable up to ten years after production ceases as a general guide. But directly they become tricky to find prices drop.

Traditional Good Times for Car Sales

The second hand market is 'keyed' to the new car market. When *new* sales are at their highest level the number of second hand sales will be correspondingly increased. Almost without exception each *new* car sale releases a second hand car which has to be sold and so on, in turn, to the end of the line (the scrap heap!). Patterns vary in different countries according to weather conditions (if they tend to be extreme), when most people are likely to go on their holidays (they keep their money for the holiday!), and such like. In Great Britain the best period has usually been from March to June.

Part Exchanges

Convenience seems to be the main attraction of part exchange but you can pay heavily for such convenience! The apparent simplicity of the deal and the slick 'helping you out of trouble sir', approach of the salesman often cloud the real issues of price.

To see where you really stand it is essential to evaluate the

18

true market price of the car you are selling and then do the same for the one you are being offered. Work out the difference and that should be the amount of cash to change hands on the deal! Better to sell your car elsewhere (if your evaluation was right!) than to pay much 'convenience' loss on a deal. (See page 83 regarding H.P. commission.)

Dealer's Profit
A dealer has to make a profit on your old car and it is a mistake to grudge it to him. He therefore has to buy your car somewhat *under* the retail market value.

He takes a risk putting money into your car for an unknown length of time before he can re-sell it. Money tied up is expensive with high interest rates prevailing. The car fills a space in the showroom and has to earn the overhead costs applicable to that space during the time its hangs fire awaiting sale. There will probably be advertising costs. Restoration work may need doing to a greater extent than you thought. He may have to guarantee the car for three months in order to command a good price and take the risk no major faults come to light during that period.

Value Added Tax will have to be added to the difference between what he pays you for the car and its final selling price. His costs of repairs are *not* deductible, when calculating this mark up amount upon which VAT is charged.

If you feel the dealer's profit or the VAT should be in your pocket, then become a private seller! This is a personal choice. But in making it it is worth remembering that if you are to do the selling it will be *your* capital that will be tied up at risk if prices plunge, *you* will have to spend time and money on advertising, *you* will have to stay home when a prospective buyer *says* he will come (they frequently fail to turn up), *you* who will have to carry on insuring and taxing the car. Is it worth it?

If you can match the salesmanship of the professional, it could be (you may learn something from page 71 about selling). To a high salary earner it is almost certainly not worth it. But it may be worth the time and trouble to someone who is retired or on low income, provided he can afford the capital. However he can get round the latter difficulty to some extent by selling first.

The dealer tends to require more profit percentage-wise on a cheap car than on an expensive one. This is because the overheads for the space the car will occupy and his sales staff, will be much the same whatever the car. His costs bulk larger compared to the total price. Thus he may look for say, £100 profit on a car he buys for £400 (25 per cent) but only £225 profit on a model bought for £1,500 (15 per cent). Thus you stand a better chance of doing well by selling a cheap car privately than you would with an expensive one.

Guarantees

If you are buying a good car, which you should be able to judge with the help of the next chapter, a guarantee is not going to be worth much, if anything to you except for peace of mind. So why pay more for it? Unless the guarantee covers parts, labour – *everything* – the garage can wriggle anyway. And I can assure you you won't win. It's a case of what comes off here goes on there. A garage will only sell a car with a warranty if it is pretty certain it won't go wrong within the brief guarantee period anyway. Another reason why guarantees are a flimsy safeguard is that the customer is *already protected* under the Sale of Goods Act and The Trade Descriptions Act. More of this in the legal chapter (Chapter 5).

Once you have decided the price is right and fair the real question you must ask yourself is 'Do I trust this firm to put things right if they go wrong?' If you can't trust the salesman my advice is not to trust the firm either because no good firm allows second-raters to stay around long. Your best guide as to the type of firm it is is likely to be a friend (with wide experience of running cars and what things ought to cost) who has had satisfactory dealings with them over a long period.

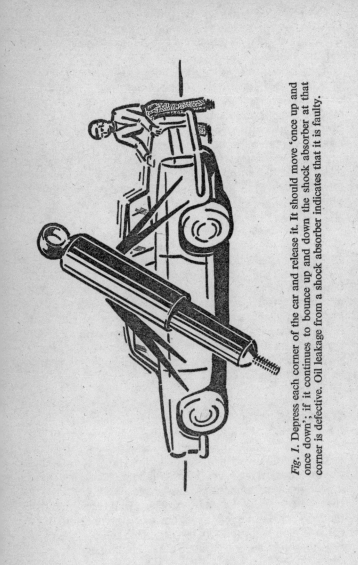

Fig. 1. Depress each corner of the car and release it. It should move 'once up and once down'; if it continues to bounce up and down the shock absorber at that corner is defective. Oil leakage from a shock absorber indicates that it is faulty.

The rough diamond type of dealer knows how to run rings around the law and has plenty of tricks up his sleeve with which to get out of fulfilling any guarantee he gives.

Nevertheless a fair guarantee, even if it only covers parts and not labour, may be allowed to tip the balance in favour of one of two similar cars *at the same price* if the other carries little or no guarantee. Provided the dealer's reputation is sound and supported by your investigations as to how his guarantees work out in practice you will be best advised to plump for the guaranteed vehicle.

A dealer cannot increase the car's price much on account of his guarantee without suffering against lower priced competition. So although you won't be getting anything for nothing, you will get good value from an honest guarantee.

Because disreputable traders also give (disreputable) guarantees, the better dealers are forced to give a good guarantee. This is why market prices tend to be guarantee inclusive and why your judgement of the firm concerned is so important. The majority of buyers amongst the public are unable to discern the difference between a sound guarantee and a worthless piece of paper, and enquiring around a little before parting with your money can pay you handsome dividends. If the dealer goes broke, note that your guarantee would become valueless, unless you were hoping to frame it as a collector's item!

Hire Purchase

The *cost* of hire purchasing must be looked at separately from the cash price of the car which we have so far been comparing. Some hire purchase arrangements are good value, others are hideously expensive compared to alternative methods for raising cash. As will be examined in Chapter 4, it is the total amount you will have paid when the H.P. contract concludes that matters. This can be compared with the cash price of the car to see the true cost of the H.P. The car salesman will probably be pleased to sell you the car on H.P. because he will collect a fat commission from the finance company for introducing the business (see also page 83). For this reason he may not be too keen for you to perceive the real cost of the H.P. contract!

Glass's Guide

This Guide book of car values has been published every month for over a quarter of a century and is sold by subscription only to members of the motor trade and a small number of other people, such as the hire purchase companies, who can show that they have a *bona fide* reason for wanting it. It is *not* available to the general public. Over the years it has become widely recognized as the motor trader's reference 'bible' on current prices, in Great Britain.

Using information drawn from dealers all over the country the guide shows each month prices for practically all types of car. A buying price and a selling price is given for every model for *each calendar year registration* so that, for instance, a two-year-old example will be marked with higher buying and selling values than a three-year-old one.

The prices are set to allow for an average mileage of around 10,000–12,000 miles per year and they assume average condition. Although the prices given are only intended to be a *guide* it is a fact that the majority of dealers work strictly to the book, making allowances for exceptionally good (or bad) condition and unusually high (or low) mileage.

'Part exchange' prices are not published in the Guide. This is because they vary considerably from dealer to dealer according to his new car stock position at any one time and the desirability of the part exchange car.

Glass's Guide can fairly be described as the sheet anchor of market prices. Without it dealers would have no reference point for their guidance: a buoyant, steady, competitive market would be almost impossible. And an efficiently organized, well informed market is just as essential to the private individual as it is to the trade.

Road Tax Disc

Many owners give this away without thinking. Unless a

prospective buyer is prepared to pay whatever it is still worth on top of the agreed price for the car you should send it back and get the refund, but, if it is on the car when the deal is agreed then it becomes the buyer's property from that moment. You cannot slip it off afterwards which at the least would be an underhand trick and would probably be properly regarded as theft.

2

Assessing Mechanical and Body Condition

In this chapter we are concerned with the condition of the car. This is the great question mark that hangs over the used car. On it depends the price to be paid, or if there is to be a sale at all.

The condition of a car can be found out exactly by taking it to pieces and making a minute examination and measurement of all the parts, as is in fact done when London buses are reconditioned.

Like most ideals, this is not practicable. Instead we must substitute an estimate based upon the examination of the car as it stands. How accurate the estimate will be depends upon the care, knowledge and experience used to arrive at it – and the time available. The time is usually limited. We can only expect the seller to allow reasonable examination and other work of assessment. There is a point beyond which patience will be strained.

Clearly if the car is not old and is in excellent condition, the price will be high so a much more careful examination would be justified and would be accepted. If the car is an old one, and therefore cheap, the situation is different. No lengthy period of assessment is justified. However, to the man who can only afford a cheap car, the importance of getting the best car he can for his money may be as great or greater than in the case of a man who is looking for a near new model.

We are concerned with everything that affects the condition of the car, and this means not just the car itself. The ever present risk in buying a second hand car is very closely related to the kind of person who has used it, or who has it for sale.

Sometimes you can get a very good idea of what condition the car is likely to be in by assessing the character and purpose of the man who is selling it. This requires a rather uncommon shrewdness.

I once bought a car after a casual visual examination. The car was advertised and seemed to be cheap for the year so I went to see it. It turned out it was a girl who had it. She was a typist. She asked if I would like to try it and I suggested she should give me a short run in it. While doing it she said she had had the clutch done, the brakes done and mentioned one or two other things.

I asked if anyone else had been to see it. No, she said, but she had a friend at work who was going to bring a friend to see it. She mentioned one or two slight defects. I asked what she was going to do without the car. 'I would like a Mini, and I will get one but I would like to wait for an 'X' registration (the new suffix letter, then about due).

I was satisfied that she knew of no fault in the car that she had not mentioned. I knew the engine was smooth and the transmission seemed to be in order. The appearance was good. I said I would take it. She then pointed out a bad oil leakage from the engine.

She kindly agreed to deliver the car on Sunday evening. When she did it was clean inside and out. It contained some tools, a starting handle, a jack and the maker's handbook.

The water pump failed the following day, but she could have had no inkling that it was about to happen. The car proved to be a good 'buy' – excellent value for the price paid for it.

I bought this car mainly on my assessment of the seller. It was a calculated risk which I cheerfully accepted and it paid off. Now, I am not suggesting that this is the method the

26

Fig. 2. Water leakage at the windscreen or other similar points can be difficult to cure.

reader should use when buying a car. What I do say is that the condition of the car can to some extent be evaluated from the kind of person that is selling it. There are high risk sellers and low risk sellers.

Who are the high risk sellers? There is the motoring enthusiast whose car is his toy. He has some part of it in pieces every weekend, and maybe, every night. He is an endless tinkerer and his car is never right. If a car is advertised as 'enthusiastically maintained' this can often be translated as 'systematically wrecked'.

On the other hand there are knowledgeable and experienced car enthusiasts who have good workshop facilities – but their work is always serious; they do not tinker. There are not many of these, and they should be accepted only on their reputation.

If I say do not buy a car from a farmer, I malign farmers generally (so far as cars are concerned) and taking farmers individually, this obviously cannot always be true. None the less it is very often true that farmers badly misuse their cars, by undermaintenance (or no maintenance at all) overloading and general misuse. The extremely unkempt condition of such cars when they are not for sale but in daily use is evidence enough of the treatment they receive. Maybe, on occasions, a car of this kind will be cleaned up and offered for sale. Evidence of such neglect is fortunately virtually impossible to eradicate.

Then there is the dealer in a small way – a part-timer who buys cars 'does them up' and sells them. Probably he only sells one car a month or less. He aims to make as much profit as possible from every deal and therefore will only do work that is essential to make the car saleable. This may involve disguising faults long enough to deceive a buyer. He may have connections with or even a job in the motor trade giving him access to sources where he can obtain suitable cars to sell himself 'on the side'.

When you go to see a car, note if there are any other cars about or any signs of a makeshift workshop; if there are you should see the red light.

There are other ways of detecting such people. You will be keeping an eye on the classified advertisements. Usually cars are advertised to a telephone number. An often repeated number over the weeks with a different car for sale denotes a dealer.

When such a number answers you, why not say 'Is the car you are advertising still for sale?' I did this once and the reply was 'H'm, Ahmm ... which one?' Obviously he was a dealer. If I had mentioned the name of the car I was enquiring about, I would not have been provided with this information. There is no point in paying a fat profit to such people, and buying trouble.

What about women and cars? Cars are often advertised as 'One lady owner' or 'Wife's car'. It is quite common for a dealer to mention that the previous owner of the car was a girl. Clearly all this is considered as an inducement to purchase. There is something in it, but not always.

Women do not in general drive cars as hard as men do, and they usually tot up a much smaller mileage over a similar period. To their credit also stands the fact that they do not generally tinker with their cars. Of course, the boy friend or husband can fully nullify this excellent feminine trait.

The female mind is usually singularly detached from all mechanical things and may ignore vital needs, such as a man would hardly ever do. They can run out of water, fuel and sometimes oil, and one never can be sure what might not have happened at some time to lay the seeds, the tares of which must in due course be reaped. The story of the lady who went to the dealer she bought a new car from and complained that the dipstick was not long enough to reach the oil might be true!

A well-to-do woman will usually have her car serviced regularly. On the whole, if a woman has been running cars for a considerable length of time, there is no 'male assistance' and no obvious sign of trouble, the 'Woman's car' is probably a better risk than most. It may be that a woman is more likely to tell the truth about the car than a man.

Professional people nearly always trade-in their cars when they are buying a new one. But this is not always so. Doctor, dentist, lawyer – such people do not usually keep a car until it is old, and they very seldom tinker with their cars. Often they sense trouble quickly, are experienced with the behaviour of cars, and seek expert advice at once. We need hardly point out there are exceptions to every rule.

There is the question of the number of previous owners. This must be important. There is a saying that when you get three people together, one of them is often a fool. This would make two fools in half a dozen owners, and to buy a car that only one fool had anything to do with is bad enough. As in all other things chance plays a big part. All of six previous owners may have been outstandingly good. One bad owner may rapidly undo all the care of the previous owners. You cannot know them all, and unless you do you cannot judge.

Certainly there are some people who age a car at a quite astounding rate. Such owners can usually be identified simply by relating the age of the car to its appearance. There are odd car people whose cars seem to have an unsatiable appetite for such 'trifles' as gearboxes, engines and back axles and sundry other components. It would be better for all concerned if they would 'call it a day' and have done with cars for good. In this way the unfortunate people who sell cars to them, repair or make cars for them and, perhaps above all, buy cars from them, would sleep more peacefully in their beds and awake to happier days.

Don't forget the freak one-owner car, the salesman who knocks up a huge mileage each year, or perhaps a car hire operator selling a car he no longer wants – and there are others.

Then there is the affluent tear-away youth who 'knocks hell' out of a car in one year and then passes on to pastures new. He knows all the faults of different models because he has discovered most of them in a very short time and has added not a few of his own. Very often the car's appearance belies its usage. This sort of chap pays well for his pleasure. So do those who buy his cast-offs.

Perhaps finally we should consider the question 'why do people sell cars?' In selling a car most people will give a reason for ridding themselves of something which they hope is sufficiently valuable to arouse the desire of possession in someone else. There are many reasons.

1. The owner may no longer be able to run a car, and so he has to sell.
2. The owner may have decided that his improved

finances have placed him in a position where he can afford a better car.

3. The car may be giving so much trouble that he wants rid of it.

4. The owner may think (or be sure) that an expensive repair is just round the corner.

5. The owner may be a wealthy person who may indulge his fancy by changing his car often.

6. The dealer. The dealer sells cars to make money. He sells no bargains; bargains are things he hopes to buy. A good dealer will not knowingly sell a faulty car. There are many dealers who are not good. The good ones usually only sell expensive cars, often well outside the price range of the lower bracket buyer.

7. Sometimes the 'company car' is replaced at a certain mileage. Such a car may or may not be well maintained. It is not generally a good buy. But companies do sometimes have other reasons which result in a car in superb condition being sold off quickly at the current price. For example, their financial year may be ending and they want to spend out on a new car (or cars) before the tax man lays his hand on the profits. Again, in these days of distorted values, it could be simply that an employee has to be given a bigger, better model in order to retain his services.

8. Some firms in the motor trade will run their cars only within the guarantee period. These cars are sold off at intervals as 'nearly new' or 'demonstrator' bargains. They sell on their impeccable appearance, but the price asked is usually very high, representing poor value.

9. The owner may simply have found his family getting too big for the car, perhaps with holidays looming up.

Certainly it is worth carefully considering the reason the seller gives for wanting to sell the car. A good and valid reason for selling may give the car a hall mark. You may know a friend's car, for example, and why he is selling it.

There are other instances when the history of the car and its owner are fully known. But of course it is rare to be in a position to buy a used car in these circumstances.

The Price Plus

It is reasonable to assume that when you buy a used car you will have to spend some extra money on it. The older the car is the more money you are likely to have to spend. It is true, we can conjure up in our imagination the perfectly maintained car, and if we can buy one we should have little or nothing to spend on it for some time. Such cars do exist. They are few and far between.

There is always the possibility that you will have to meet the cost of rectifying some serious defect soon after you buy the car, an unfortunate fortuitous coincidence, not detectable and suspected by anyone. Such things happen to a new car, though there the guarantee comes to the rescue.

Some expenses can however, be clearly foreseen. If the tyres are worn, you will need a new set, or soon will, and this will be a sizeable increase in the price of the car. You may need a new battery. Anything that doesn't work will have to be put right, and unless you can put it right yourself, it will cost money. Electrical trouble can be expensive. Therefore bear in mind the cost of all replacements and repairs that will be necessary.

Look out for tyre damage and uneven tyre wear. (See Fig. 17.) Signs of underinflation also probably mean serious damage to the tyre wall, which can only be seen from the inside. Any visible exterior damage to the tyre walls, tears or 'swellings' indicate serious damage probably due to 'kerbing' (allowing the tyre to bump against the kerb). Such a tyre is a 'write off' however sound the tread may be. Check the *inward* facing tyre walls for this sort of trouble.

In the U.K. *more* than one millimetre (1/25 inch) of tread depth must be present on at least three quarters of the entire tread. No bulges or slits are allowed on the walls, nor are cuts of more than one inch across the tread area (or of more than ten per cent of the tread width). It is illegal to use tyres

32

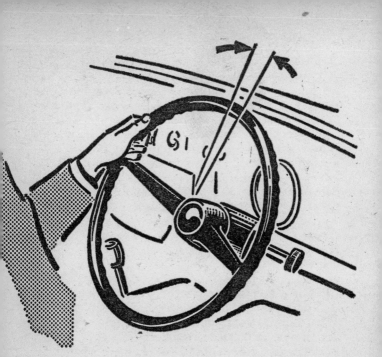

Fig. 3. With the front wheels in the 'straight ahead' position, check the steering wheel for 'free movement' by turning it in both directions, as shown. If it is as much as 1½ inches it is at the limit of permissible wear.

with any of these faults. A car sold with such a tyre would place the seller in at least a doubtful legal position.

The Body

The condition of the body is vital. A sound body may merit a reconditioned engine or gearbox, or other major replacement but a body that is riddled with corrosion – the car cancer – puts the car on the scrap heap.

Appearance has a very significant relationship with price. This must be obvious but unfortunately appearance can be created on a very insecure foundation – a rotted body. Such doctoring will not deceive the experienced eye, but it can look very good.

It is possible to make a very good guess at the condition of a car generally, by the appearance of the body. It is unusual to find that a car has been well used and maintained and the body neglected. Contrary wise a body that shows clear evidence of neglect can be taken to indicate a similar mechanical neglect. This is a pretty safe bet. Of course a lot can be done to spruce a car up for the eye of a possible buyer but real neglect is difficult, if not impossible to eradicate. A possible exception to this rule is the car that has covered a very great mileage in a short time.

A re-spray can boost a car's appearance sky high. It can be a good thing or a bad thing; it all depends on why it was done. The usual reasons are:

1. The owner thinks he would like a change of colour – a not uncommon reason.
2. Simply to improve the appearance of the car – to restore shine that time has dulled.
3. The repair of accident damage has made a re-spray essential. Usually the whole car is not resprayed to cover accident damage repairs. Therefore a partial re-spray is nearly conclusive evidence that the car has been in an accident.
4. Repairs to body corrosion damage have made a re-spray necessary.

You can always detect a re-spray. If done recently there is likely to be some of the colour on the tyres. Look under the window rubbers. Look round the inside of the boot and bonnet. Careful inspection will reveal a re-spray. The colour of the car should correspond with the colour stated in the log book. If it has been done simply to improve the appearance of the car it is a good thing and to be regarded as an asset, but in this case it will not be newly done. No one (except perhaps a dealer who has the facilities) will re-spray a car just to sell it. It would be suspicious to say the least if a car that had just been re-sprayed was offered for sale by anyone other than a dealer.

Reasons 3 and 4 are ominous. It is true that if accident damage is properly repaired the car is still sound but, and it is a big 'but', such repairs are often not properly carried out. There may be a reduction in strength or there may be mis-alignment of the body. Even slight misalignment will affect tyre wear. In such a 'botched' repair it may have been found that the car 'feels' better when the toe-in is incorrectly adjusted. If, after the car has been bought, the steering is correctly adjusted the fault comes to light. Such a fault is virtually incurable because of the very extensive work that would be required to correct the steering angles.

There is a considerable trade done in insurance 'write offs'. In certain media you will find lists of almost new cars with 'front end damage' or 'rear end damage'; all are stated to be repairable. They are all cheap enough for anyone with the necessary facilities to repair and sell at a profit. As discussed later we are not in favour of them, even though when satisfactory repair job has been made, such cars should suffer at least a 30 per cent reduction in what would otherwise be their market value. Unfortunately in most cases, the buyer is unaware of the true situation and pays the full price.

Reason 4 covers the doctored car. Often a bad body is made to look like a very good one. Holes due to corrosion are filled with fibre glass or other suitable substances and the surfaces are smoothed down so that when the finish is finally applied an 'as new' lustre appears.

This kind of body repair is easily detected with a magnet. You can buy a small, powerful magnet at model shops. A magnet will stick to the body, if there is steel under the finish, but not to a filling. Try the magnet first on a part of the body that is sound and note how strongly it is attracted by the steel. A *thin* filling will noticeably reduce the pull of the magnet, though it may still stick, but a filling of any thickness will prevent the magnet holding at all. With the magnet you can check the extent of the corrosion by moving it around the parts where corrosion is most likely to be found.

Cars differ greatly in the way they corrode, some are good and some are very bad; this is reflected in the second hand market prices. All car firms employ experts in metal technology who are well versed in all the aspects of corrosion and yet cars are produced with construction faults from the corrosion aspect that must unnecessarily reduce the life of the car. Pockets are left where mud can gain access and accumulate when this could easily have been avoided. Thick accumulations of mud take a long time to dry out and thus speed up corrosion. This is a situation accentuated by the salt put on the roads in the Winter. One must assume there is a certain amount of 'built in obsolescence' when construction techniques are used which result in unnecessarily rapid corrosion. Some cars are very much better than others from the corrosion point of view and it is well worth bearing this in mind when buying a car.

Rolls-Royce use stainless steel for their exhaust systems and galvanized steel for the body. It has been calculated that the cost of using galvanized steel in the popular car would be less than £3. The thickness of the zinc coating required is only two or three thousands of an inch and this would extend body life 3 to 4 fold, *without any other added protection.* If a car made in this way was undersealed and the body cavities injected with rust inhibitor the body would have an indefinite life.

Places to look for corrosion are shown in the illustrations.

Some used car dealers re-spray all the cars they take in above a certain grade, whenever the great improvement in appearance justifies the cost. The result is a considerable upward boost in the price. Such a re-spray may be an inferior one. It is a practice not generally in the interests of the buyer.

36

Fig. 4. Look for deep corrosion round the spring mountings. These mountings often push right through into the car when corrosion is extreme.

The Mileage

Mileage is a magic word to many who are seeking a used car, but it may mean little or nothing. Even if true, the mileage that a car has covered tells only part of the story but, the usage that the car has received has a significant bearing on its condition. This is often overlooked.

The mileage can be and sometimes is doctored. If the recorded mileage is less than 10,000 per year and there is no reason known why it should be so low, there is cause for suspicion. In some cases the mileage may be high but a reconditioned engine is said to have been fitted. This might increase the price, though proof that the engine had been fitted and proof of the date when it was fitted would be necessary. Bear in mind that a new engine does not rejuvenate an old car. A car with a good engine but a bad body is still a scrap car. In such a case, unless steps are taken to reduce body corrosion in a car that has worn out one engine, the body may not last half the life of the new engine.

It is virtually impossible accurately to match the mileage to the car. How can you tell if 10,000–15,000 have been 'knocked off' when the car seems about right for 40,000?

The recorded mileage is most likely to be tampered with when the car is a nearly new one that has covered a high mileage in a short time, but there may be some evidence to suggest that there has been some 'clocking back'.

Tell tale signs can give away a clocked car. Look for undue perishing of the wiper blades. Check if the rubbers on the foot pedals are worn thinner than might be expected. Has the driver's seat springing suffered heavily? Are the window winders stiff indicating long term rusting inside the door panels? Perhaps there is a lot of slack in their action. The engine exhaust manifold becomes pitted with long use next to the engine itself and shows its age to the experienced eye. In many cars there is a fair sized space between the front grill and the engine radiator if it is front mounted. By peering inside an astute detective may learn a lot. If you have a look at some friend's cars before setting out to buy your own, you will get a good idea of what things should look like at various ages.

A car which has been rebuilt from two crashed halves of the same model can be detected by running your hand along the headlining inside, about the middle of the car. You cannot see anything from looking at the top of the roof but underneath, concealed by the headlining, will be an unusually large bump all the way across where the two halves were welded together.

The car handbook (if available) will list the standard and any optional tyres. Almost any reference library will have car specification books covering past and current models of all makes. So you can check if the tyres are likely to be the original set. Check all the wheels *including* the spare.

In *any* used car there must be *some* evidence of wear so that anything that seems 'too good to be true' is suspicious. The carpets and other floor covering, for example, even in a low mileage car must show some evidence that the car has seen some use, particularly below the accelerator pedal. If there is none, removable rubber mats have probably been used. If doubt arises in this way be doubly cautious.

If you can get a description of the car in a letter from the seller, year, mileage and so on and you can afterwards *prove* that the information is false you can probably successfully sue whoever sold you the car. (See page 89.) For log book frauds etc., see Chapter 5.

Accessories

Masses of extra driving lamps, and gadgets generally, can be regarded purely as a liability and if the seller thinks they are worth anything he should be invited to remove and keep them. They will usefully serve him again as encumbrances on his next car.

If you do get a car cluttered up by an immature enthusiast the best thing to do is to remove the stuff and dump it in the rubbish bin, where it belongs. The added lamps usually overload the electrical system and frequently cause damage. Often they are poorly wired up and constitute a risk to the wiring. It is a good rule not to fit anything to a car that does not serve as *useful purpose*. It follows that anything that is fitted that serves no useful purpose should be removed.

The Underside

It is true to say that nobody should ever buy a used car without having a look at the underside. If the car has been accidentally damaged or suffers from corrosion the cat is out of the bag when you see the underside of the car. In any case it is important to examine the underside of the car in good light so that it can be seen in detail. The ideal is to run the car over a pit, but it will do if one end of the car is run up on ramps. *A word of warning!* Do not get underneath the car when it is held only by a jack or jacks. You may lift the car by jacks so that you can get underneath it, but before you do the car must be supported very securely; use secure stands or substantial wood blocks. Do not use supports built up with bricks or planks of wood.

If only the front wheels are lifted the parking brake (after checking that it works properly) must be applied and the rear-wheels must be *securely* chocked. If you lift the rear wheels you *must* first carefully chock the front wheels so that the car cannot move.

If the car is an old one there will obviously be some corrosion. Carefully check the extent of this – will repairs be necessary? Examine the brake piping; is it corroded so that it will need to be renewed?

You may find that the car has been undersealed, and this would be a considerable advantage. Even if the underseal has been in position for a long time and has deteriorated, it must have prevented a lot of corrosion and the condition of the car must be much better than it otherwise would have been.

The Engine

While the condition of the engine is not so important as the condition of the body, it is after all the thing that makes the car go, and repairs to it are likely to be expensive unless they are trivial. Of course, if the engine is in bad condition but the rest of the car is sound, you could quite easily buy at a price that would justify fitting a replacement engine. But note that a *high performance* engine may have a replacement cost of four or five times that of a normal one – making the economics totally different.

As an engine gets older it tends to get noisier. Now, when we talk about noise in this context we don't mean exhaust noise. We mean the general mechanical noise the engine makes when it is running. Listen carefully to a good engine – it purrs smoothly and quietly – and it does this from the time you start it to the time you stop it.

Now listen to a very worn engine – behind the purr of the engine running there is considerable background noise. If it happens to be an air cooled engine it will be very noisy. If you give the engine a 'burst' of revs the noise will be accentuated as the level drops back.

There may be knocks, due to main bearing or big end wear. Noise due to a big end wear is like a clatter or 'rattle' which disappears when the engine is pulling hard under

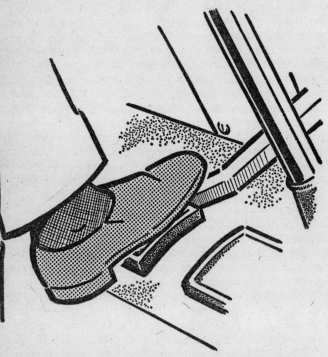

Fig. 5. Check for 'free movement' in the clutch pedal. There must be some, but there should be a lot of movement between the clutch 'engaged' and clutch 'disengaged' positions. If the pedal must be depressed on to the floor to disengage the clutch, this would probably mean a worn clutch or thrust release bearing, or both.

load. The noise due to main bearing wear is more of a rumbling or thumping sound, not that it matters very much since either fault is so serious that in most cases it will end further interest in the car. Noise due to big end wear is usually at its worst just after starting the engine following a rest. The sound may be present all the time, or as you drive, it may be sometimes worse, sometimes better. You may notice the noise only fleetingly immediately after the engine is started – it is there and then disappears. This is the thin end of the wedge, the initial warning of serious bearing trouble. It is the pink light that will soon turn red. It may well be this that put the 'for sale' ticket on the car. Don't let the sales talk cover up the noise by distracting you the first time the engine is started, or the second!

When the engine has been standing idle for some time the oil, always present in the bearings, partially flows out, but in a tight bearing very little oil can leave the bearings. Not the same in a worn bearing, where the clearance between the parts is much greater and so much more of the oil does flow out. At the instant the engine starts it knocks because of the excessive play in the bearings, but, as the oil from the pump again enters the bearings, it acts as a cushion and the knock disappears. However, once an engine has reached this state it will not be long before the knock is heard at other times and finally, is always present.

The oil pump pumps oil through the bearings under pressure. The oil escapes through the normal clearance always present in the bearings and returns to the sump to be re-circulated. As the bearing clearances become greater so the oil can flow through them more easily and therefore the oil pressure from the pump drops. If the lubrication system is fitted with an oil pressure gauge this drop in pressure can be observed. When due to bearing wear it takes place over a very long period. Such a drop in pressure is virtually a certain indication of big end and/or main bearing wear.

We are not talking here about the variation in oil pressure that takes place as the engine heats up, but the steady pressure when the engine is at normal running temperature. You can find what the correct pressure should be from the makers' service manual, or perhaps from a friend who runs the same model.

Remember the pressure does vary slightly from one engine to another even when they are new, but such a difference would only be a pound or two and is not important, it is a *big drop* we are looking for.

Unfortunately few cars are fitted with an oil pressure gauge, but all are fitted with an oil pressure warning light. This light should go out *immediately* the engine starts, if it lingers the oil pressure is low, particularly at the instant the engine starts because the pump has had to fill the excessive clearance in the worn bearings.

It is true to say that no knock is good, but it is also true to say that all knocks are not very bad.

The engine may appear to have a loud knock, due to a faulty water pump, or fan drive belt.

If you are not sure where the knock is coming from, press your hand firmly on the alternator (or dynamo) and if a knock is present you should feel it. Do the same with the water pump. *Do be careful not to get your hand, face, or tie in the fan – it's an accident that happens so often.*

To check the fan drive if it is almost certain it is the source of a knock, either remove the belt or slacken it off so much that it does not drive the fan. You can run the engine for a *short* time without the fan turning, in fact you need do little more than start the engine and stop it. Make sure you adjust the belt correctly afterwards. The present owner should not object to this check being made because a knock is present and you are simply trying to discover if it is a serious one or not, *but you must have his clear permission.* Best to have a witness too, because if the car went wrong next day he might blame you and try to land you in court! THE SAME APPLIES TO ANY OTHER TESTS YOU MAY DO TO SOMEONE'S CAR.

Do not forget that the knock may not be in the engine at all. If the knock is present only when the car is on the move, disappearing when the car is stopped but with the engine running, then the knock is not in the engine.

Excessive smoking of the exhaust is a sign that something serious is wrong. It may be a sign of worn cylinder bores, and it is best to assume that this is the cause. It may just be due to broken piston rings or to rings stuck in their grooves with carbon, but even if this is the case the remedy would be expensive. You can confirm the bad news from the exhaust by finding out if the compression is poor.

You can check the compression quite easily if you have a starting handle. Have the engine at normal operating temperature and the *ignition switched off*. Turn the engine slowly by means of the handle. You will feel resistance as each piston overcomes the compression; the engine will turn in a series of 'bumps', each 'bump' being the resistance offered by the compression to the piston in one of the cylinders. The resistance of each 'bump' should be about the same and each 'bump' should be evenly spaced. If the resistance seems to vary, weak in some cases, strong in others, the compression in some of the cylinders is weak. If the 'bumps' are unevenly spaced, it is probable that one or more of the cylinders have no compression at all.

In cars where a starting handle cannot be used, engage top gear (ignition off), and jack up one of the driving wheels and turn this by hand to compare the 'bumps'. Even by pushing the car in top gear (*ignition off*) you will have some indication if the compression is good or bad. If you can make a comparison by making the same test on another car of the same kind, known to be in good condition, you will be better able to judge the state of the compression in the car being tested.

Remember, all defects must be related to the cost of having them repaired *at a garage*. If the estimated cost of a repair is £15 and you are in the happy position of being able to do the job yourself, or have someone do it for you for £5, the full £15 must still be deducted from the price of the car for a fair valuation.

The Drive Differential Unit

If the car has front wheel drive this will be at the front of the car. Differential trouble is not common, but if present, it is very serious. Symptoms would normally be a rumble, less likely a whine, but either would be a very bad sign.

In front wheel drive cars there is the additional possibility of wear in the universal joints which may give rise to the 'knock on lock' symptom – a knock which occurs only when the wheels are turned from the straight ahead position. Such a knock should be listened for when rounding corners.

Wear in the Universal joints in the propeller shaft leading to the differential in rear drive cars may be detected by holding the shaft and trying to shake it vigorously. Wear in such a joint may be detected by inserting a screwdriver and using it as a lever to try and produce movement in the joint. Any movement would indicate wear.

The Gearbox

What we look for in the gearbox is the smooth selection of all the gears and that the mechanism never slips out of a gear by itself. Difficulty in selecting gears, assuming the clutch is not at fault, would probably be because of a faulty synchro-mesh mechanism and this would be an expensive repair. A continuous whine in the gearbox while driving indicates incorrect meshing of the gear teeth due to bearing wear. All gearbox repairs are expensive.

Steering

Here we look for excessive free play in the steering due to wear. You can get a fair idea of what the steering is like by having the front wheels in the straight ahead position and then lightly turning the steering wheel first one way and then the other, as far as it will go in each direction *but without turning the wheels.* This test shows the free play in the steering. The movement should be less than $1\frac{1}{2}$ inches. If greater movement than this is present there is excessive wear in the steering gears, in the steering linkage or in both, and the car would fail its D.O.E. (formerly M.O.T.) test.

Wear in the steering gearbox or rack and pinion, whichever type is fitted can often be taken up by means of an adjustment provided for this purpose, so this may not be a serious fault, but find out about adjustment possibilities.

The best way to check steering is to get under the car (when it is properly supported and in good light) and observe the action of the steering parts when the steering wheel is moved just sufficiently to take up the free play. It should be possible to see or feel wear in the ball joints, that is free movement before the wheels begin to move. Steering faults are very likely to show up in the road test.

Brakes
When you put your foot on the brake pedal and press, it should have a 'hard' feel. If it feels spongy or springy a fault is present. Such a fault may be due to air in the hydraulic system and this is easily cured by bleeding the system. The fault could be caused by a loose mounting of the master cylinder. Poor brakes are usually due to lack of adjustment or worn linings. Re-lining the brakes all round can be quite expensive. The thickness of the lining of the pads of disc brakes may be inspected simply by removing the cover, if one is present, and looking at the side of the pads. When the lining has worn down to 1/16 inch replacement pads will be *essential* immediately.

Suspension
The characteristics of different suspension systems differ very considerably and what would be recognized as a fault in one system would be normal in another but, of course, there are certain forms of behaviour that must be classified as a fault in any system.

Clearly, for example, if the car is not level when it is on a level road (down on one side) there is something wrong. This is usually the symptom of a tired leaf spring – a leaf spring that after long use has lost its shape.

To put this right requires a new spring, and then very likely the car will be slightly 'up' on the side that was low

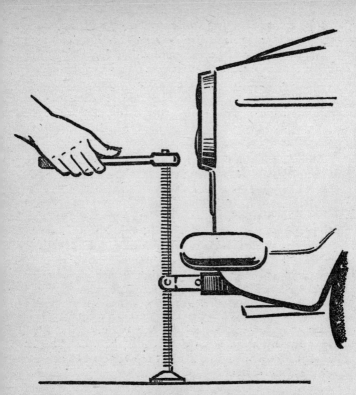

Fig. 6. Have the owner place the jack under each of the jacking points in turn and lift the car. In a badly corroded body the jacking points will not withstand the pressure and will move upwards into the body. You *must* ask the present owner to do this because if any damage does come to light, or occur, it will be of his own making, and not yours.

because it is probable that the other spring has acquired some 'set'.

Another way to cure this trouble is to have the old spring set up by a blacksmith. Blacksmiths are more or less non-existent nowadays but most large towns have a firm who specialize in this sort of work. In this case you could have both springs treated at the same time. A broken spring would require to be renewed.

When the trouble occurs in a car fitted with torsion bar suspension it may be possible to adjust the bar to restore the car to a level condition. Pressurized suspension systems which develop this trouble may have a leakage in one unit, in which case increasing the pressure will only be a temporary cure. A new suspension unit would be very expensive.

If the suspension is very lively over bumps and bottoms on large bumps, you are safe to conclude that one or more of the shock absorbers are faulty. Generally a shock absorber becomes faulty through break down of the oil seals and consequent loss of oil. If the shock absorber is examined it will be oily.

A simple check is to depress one corner of the car heavily and then to release it suddenly. If the car moves once up, once down and stops, the shock absorber near that wheel is in order. Try all four corners of the car. If when the car is depressed and released the up and down movement continues through several up and down movements the shock absorber at that wheel is faulty.

Occasionally the rubber bush in an eye at the mounting point of a shock absorber fails so that play develops. This play will give rise to a knock. The way to check for this is to get under the car and inspect the rubber bush. The fault can usually be seen, and it should be possible to move the shock absorber sideways by pushing and pulling it. A replacement unit is the only remedy.

Rubber bushes are very widely used in all independent front wheel suspension systems and when they deteriorate the result is excessive play which is expensive to put right.

If a front wheel is jacked up clear of the ground and the wheel is then grasped top and bottom and an attempt is made to rock it by alternately pushing at the top or bottom there will be movement if wear is present in the wheel bearings, wheel swivel joints (king pins), or in the suspension linkage.

If you have someone rock the wheel as described while you watch on the inside it will be possible to see where the movement is taking place. Movement between the brake backplate and the brake drum shows that there is play in the wheel bearings. If there is play at the wheel swivel bearings this indicates wear in these bearings. Play may be seen at the suspension bearings which would, again, indicate wear.

There may be some play at all these points and if there is it it will all be added together in the movement of the wheel as it is rocked. If slight play is present, but cannot be seen, place the fingers over the joint between the brake back plate and the brake drum; the slightest play between these two parts will then be detected when the wheel is rocked. Do the same at the other points mentioned. It may be that the wheel bearings can be adjusted and therefore the excessive play eliminated. Don't forget that some play, just a trace of it, in the front wheel bearings, may be specified by the manufacturers.

Toughened Windscreens and Windows

The majority of popular cars use toughened glass windscreens and side windows. The alternative, laminated glass, is used for the windscreen on more expensive cars and many sports cars. A small scratch or two on a laminated screen will not weaken it.

Toughened glass, however, is greatly weakened by any chip or scratch. The strength of a piece of toughened glass depends on its compression skin being intact. The slightest damage to the skin is a potential source of shattering.

You should inspect the front screen thoroughly and, on the side windows, look particularly at all the exposed edges. A damaged front windscreen could be dangerous and should be replaced.

The Electrical System

Carefully check all the electrical circuits by operating the various switches. See that all these work properly: the headlights, on dipped and main beam, side and tail lights, interior lights, reversing light and direction indicators. Check also the dash panel lights and warning lights, windscreen wipers and the heater boost fan if one is fitted. Electrical repairs can be expensive and a fault in any of the lighting circuits is suspicious; it means that the car cannot have been used at night and, as few people will tolerate such a fault, it may be that there is expensive damage to the electrical wiring, which renders repair difficult and therefore expensive.

The battery is an item likely to need renewal in a used car. Battery neglect is common and makes things worse. The best check on the battery is the way it operates the starter. If the starter spins the engine really energetically there can't be much wrong with the battery.

Have a look at the battery; if it is thickly coated with dirt and connections are covered with corrosion, it is probable that most of its life is past.

If the starter operates sluggishly or that 'energetic spin' we mentioned is absent you can bank on it that a new battery is required.

The starter should operate smoothly and positively. Noisy engagement, common on old cars, is usually an indication of a worn starter ring on the flywheel, and this is expensive to put right. A common starter fault is 'spinning'; the starter runs but fails to engage; it may only do this *sometimes* so operate it more than once. A weak battery will prevent the starter operating properly. A check is to switch on the head-lamps and to watch them when the starter is operated. If the battery is in bad condition they will dim right down when the starter is operated. Even with a good battery they will dim slightly.

Publisher's note: Electrical faults can be particularly perplexing, even to experienced mechanics. B. C. Macdonald co-author of this book has written two other Paperfronts in which diagnosis of electrical faults is simplified. For the absolute beginner 'Car Repairs Properly Explained' will enable him to understand how a car works and to do more simple repairs, and for the more experienced, 'Car Doctor A–Z' shows the way. Both books have been best sellers over many years.

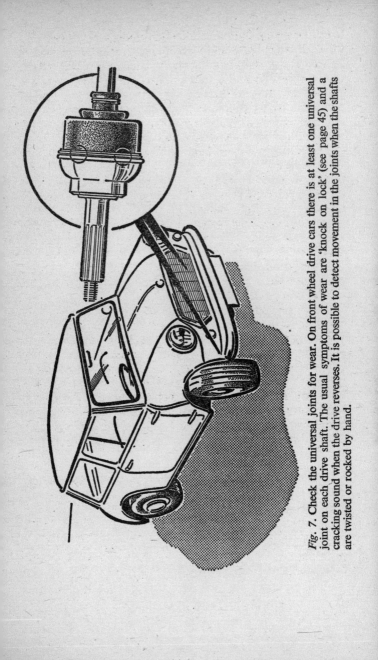

Fig. 7. Check the universal joints for wear. On front wheel drive cars there is at least one universal joint on each drive shaft. The usual symptoms of wear are 'knock on lock' (see page 45) and a cracking sound when the drive reverses. It is possible to detect movement in the joints when the shafts are twisted or rocked by hand.

Alignment

If the car has suffered accident damage and has been badly repaired it is very likely that there will be some misalignment. The makers always specify measurements between certain points which enable a check to be made on the alignment, but unless proper facilities are available these are likely to be too difficult to make.

If you turn the front wheels until they are in the straight ahead position and then lie on the ground some considerable distance behind the car you should be able to see if there is much misalignment by sighting along the wheels. Usually such misalignment will affect the steering. At some time or other you have probably noticed when following a car that its wheels are not tracked correctly, but a very considerable deviation would be necessary before it can be seen in this way. Uneven tyre wear may be caused by misalignment. (See Fig. 17.)

The Clutch

It is probably true to say that everything on the car wears, but the clutch has an exceptionally arduous task to perform and wears faster than all other parts, except, perhaps, the brakes. It is also an expensive item to have serviced. Some drivers habitually misuse the clutch, not fully understanding what it is for and how to use it properly. In such cases the clutch can wear very quickly.

What happens is that the friction linings wear away and the clutch will not engage properly because there is insufficient pedal movement. There may be adjustment to compensate for this, but ultimately the adjustment is insufficient and the clutch fails to engage correctly. Alternatively the linings are so badly worn they cannot provide sufficient friction and the clutch slips. Normally the clutch should engage when the clutch pedal is near the upper end of its travel. In a good clutch the free pedal movement, when the pedal is lightly lifted and pressed down (but not pressed sufficiently to operate the clutch) should be about $\frac{1}{2}''$. In other words, there should be *plenty* of movement when

52

you depress the pedal *after the slack has been taken up.*

Along with the clutch friction linings, another point of wear is the clutch release or thrust bearing. When a clutch friction disc is renewed it is a good thing to renew the release bearing at the same time, even if this is not strictly necessary, because if this is not done it is likely that the whole of the dismantling work necessary to service the clutch will have to be repeated at a later date, to renew a failed thrust bearing.

The D.O.E. Test

The D.O.E. test is intended to make sure that no car can be licensed unless it is safe to drive on the roads; it therefore takes account only of those things that have a bearing on safety, the tyres, the lights, steering and so on. A worn engine or gearbox would be no hindrance to the car passing the D.O.E. test. Therefore the test certificate is no criterion on which to try and estimate the price to pay for a used car. But it is important none the less because, while possession of a D.O.E. certificate far from guarantees the car to be sound, the non-possession of one is likely evidence of serious trouble.

If you are offered a car without a D.O.E. certificate, ask yourself why. Anyone with a car for sale should be prepared to obtain a D.O.E. certificate for it. If no certificate exists we can only assume this is because some unspecified trouble is present, which is probably expensive to rectify.

However, in exceptional circumstances, the car without a D.O.E. certificate may not stand condemned. If you are competent at doing your own repairs or know someone who is reliable who will do the repairs cheaply, the car could be a good 'buy'. If the car has failed to pass the test a certificate is received which describes the repairs that will be needed before a test certificate will be granted. One would not accept this as all the work that would be needed, but it is useful information and if the price is sufficiently low, say half the market value, it could still be all right.

Having said all this, if the car is offered without a test certificate, the ordinary buyer should leave it well alone.

The Test Drive

We have dealt individually with all the major parts of the car, and having read about these you will know what you are looking for during the test drive.

During the drive you should cover at least six miles and do a considerable amount of gear changing. Don't forget to travel some distance in reverse gear. Check particularly the ease the smoothness of the gear change and the operation of the clutch. Check the brakes. Do this on a road with a good dry surface and one that is clear of traffic. A tendency to pull to one side when the brakes are applied indicates uneven braking, and this could be a fault which would be fairly expensive to remedy. At low speed (10 m.p.h.) check the handbrake. While one cannot expect the handbrake, acting as it normally does on the rear wheels only, to have the same stopping power as the footbrake, it should exercise a considerable retarding effect on the car. If it appears to be weak and the lever comes well up (pawl high on ratchet) adjustment or a new cable will be required. It is true that handbrake trouble will often disappear when the wheel brakes are adjusted, but if the brake linings are worn adjustment provides no remedy. In this case and in all other instances of this kind we must assume the worst. We cannot accept the owner's assurances (unless we have good reason to believe him) on any point that may crop up during the test run that only a simple adjustment is required. If this is so, why did he not make the adjustment himself?

Notice if there is any slackness in the transmission. Accelerate; then lift your foot off the accelerator. Do this once or twice. The reversal of drive in the transmission will give rise to clicks, clacks or bangs if there is any slackness due to worn universal joints or loose bolts where rubber joints are used.

When you have come back from the test run have another

look at the engine and notice if there are any oil leaks; now is the time when they will be most easily spotted.

During the test run remember to check all the gauges. Is the ammeter (if fitted) showing that the battery is being charged? If no ammeter is fitted, does the ignition warning light go out when the engine is started and stay out until it stops or is idling slowly? Does the temperature gauge show a normal engine temperature? If the engine is overheating it may have been doing this for some time. The owner may say that it is simply due to a furred radiator and can be simply cured. Can it? De-furring compounds are effective, but often when the fur is removed leaks are uncovered and a new radiator is required. Overheating eventually leads to piston ring trouble (gummed-up rings) and is a threat to the engine generally.

We have dwelt already on the psychology of buying a used car. A good time to apply it is during the trial run. When everything is above board you are usually shown the car on the basis of 'Well, there it is'. There may be some favourable comments such as 'I've had very little trouble with it', and so on. It may be different. Note if pressure is being applied with a persistently persuasive attitude and praise of the car, and a rush to oppose criticism or minimize faults. 'That's all right, I'll fix it for you in a couple of minutes' or 'Nothing much wrong there, it's easily put right', and so on. There is a professionalism about the patter because he has done it many times before.

If the car is fairly well up the price scale the situation may be slightly different. The persuasiveness is still there. There seems to be an assumption that you will know a bargain when you see one. Any criticism of the car is received with a sort of pained disappointment, an implied criticism of yourself for failing to come up to expectations. If done properly this can make a buyer who knows little or nothing about cars feel embarrassed and it may 'bounce' him into buying the car, as it is intended to do.

If your attitude towards the car continues to be critical there is an apparent loss of interest; it becomes 'take it or leave it'. 'It is not my fault if you lose a bargain.' This is the dealer or his salesman applying his psychology of selling. If his assessment of you is that you cannot be fooled he drops on to solid earth at once and tries to switch your attention to another car.

The rogue is fairly easy to detect and you would never get as far as having a trial run with him. He is up to, and will cheerfully use all the tricks. A car's gearbox may be howling like a Banshee, but a handful of sawdust will cure that long enough for his purpose. The dynamo may be no good, but it is a simple matter to wire the ignition warning light up to the oil pressure switch to make everything seem fine. Or why not the other way? If the oil pressure is so low that the warning light has a tendency to come on, why not wire it up to the ignition warning light circuit? Such hidden faults soon come to light when it is too late.

What Sort of Car to Buy?

I have always believed that it is better to have the kind of car you want even if it means that you can't buy it new. Often the drop in price between a new and a fairly new used model makes all the difference.

A second important point is that you should buy a car that you can afford. You must be able to afford the price of the car in cash or the monthly payment. If you pay a price for the car that places an excessive restriction on your normal mode of life you make a great error, one that will deprive you of much of the pleasure possession of the car might otherwise give you. Apart from the purchase price, you must be able to afford to run the car. What is the point in having a car that has a fuel consumption so high that you have to 'think twice' every time before you use it. In such a case the fuel gauge becomes an ever painful reminder of the cost per mile that you can't afford.

These are sensible things to consider and take into account. It may be that for some personal reason that they do not all apply to you. There is always the man who is prepared to balance on the brink of bankruptcy to be able to

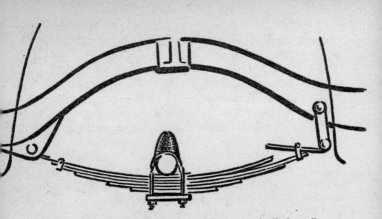

Fig. 8. Examine the springs for broken leaves (coils in coil springs). They are not always as obvious as the one shown.

run an ancient Rolls-Royce. Maybe a prestige car is essential for some reason and in the end it may justify its cost and keep. However, if your aim is to get the cheapest possible motoring and the convenience that a car provides you will 'buy within your income' and I suggest the following types of car are best left alone:

A **GT** (Grand Touring) model, because repairs are likely to be more expensive in some cases.

A sports car, because the insurance is high.

A car with an automatic gear box – if it goes wrong it will be expensive to put right.

A car with petrol injection or any car with complicated equipment of this kind because, if it goes wrong, it is expensive to put right.

Certain foreign cars, because spares are expensive and often difficult to obtain.

A car that has a low value on the used car market – because it probably has a bad reputation for corrosion or has some other fault that makes it unpopular to the used car buyer.

So You Have Bought a Used Car

When you have got the car the first thing to do when you have returned home is to check all the levels, radiator water, engine sump, gear box and drive axle, tyre pressures, etc. Make sure you know the oils and greases the makers specify and only use these. We do not refer to the *make* of lubricants, any good make will do, but the correct *grade* must be used. A hypoid differential, for example, *must* have hypoid oil.

It will take a little while to get used to the car and inevitably, if the car is of any age, there will be some apprehension – will some serious fault come to light? As the miles tot up and nothing happens confidence comes.

Often the man who has just bought a used car will set about spending his spare cash in correcting faults and generally doing what he can to improve the car. It is next to certain that the last thing he will think about is how to prevent further body corrosion. It should be the first. If he does anything at all in this direction it will be to fill in any holes, say in the sills or door panels if such holes are present. The holes are filled, smoothed, painted and all looks well, but the cause of the trouble is still there and is still as active as ever. What he has done is similar to papering over the cracks in a subsiding building. He is working on the 'out of sight out of mind' principle. The idea should be to 'stop the rot'. In truth it can't be *stopped* but it *can* be retarded. If anti-corrosion work is undertaken early enough in the car's life the body can be preserved indefinitely, but constant attention is required. The war against corrosion is never won, but it need never be lost.

Undersealing, however thoroughly done is *not enough*; it is not only the underside of the car that corrodes. All the cavities in the body are subject to corrosion, and usually this cannot be seen until it has penetrated the metal. To deal with this corrosion it is necessary to inject anti-corrosion liquid into the cavities. There are firms with depots in any fair size town who specialize in this work, but it is expensive. If the owner does the work himself it very greatly reduces the cost. The liquid used must inhibit against rust. It must also be highly penetrative (so that it will spread) and protective.

Steel used for car bodies must have a 'deep drawing' quality so that it will stretch without defects when pressed in the dies, and this steel is particularly prone to rust. Once the protective coating is penetrated rust will spread very rapidly. protective coating must consist of a rust inhibitor which is itself protected by the final finish.

Remember, if a rust patch appears the rust will spread rapidly under the finish, so that the patch to be treated is bigger than it seems to be. If such blemishes are dealt with quickly they are not noticeable and the appearance of the car is preserved.

When a rust spot appears rub all the rust away with a piece of the finest 'wet and dry' paper (obtainable at car accessory stores). Some of the finish will have to be removed in the process. Be careful, do not unnecessarily spread the damaged area. It may be that all the rust cannot be completely removed. When you have cleaned the area as well as possible paint it with 'Kurust' and allow it to dry thoroughly, then cover it with two or three coats of the final finish of the original colour of the car. Small tins of matching colour can be obtained and aerosol sprays are also obtainable.

We are talking of very small areas. Where there is a large area it would be necessary to use an undercoat and to rub this down with wet and dry paper until a perfectly smooth surface was obtained. If the surface was very rough in the first instance the rubbing will expose high points of bare metal. When this occurs more undercoat is applied and this is again rubbed down. Working in this way all the hollows that make the surface uneven are filled in and a smooth surface obtained. When the final finish is applied to such a surface it will dry smooth and glossy. Never assume you can get away without a rust inhibitor next to the bare metal. Without this protection the steel will rust again. Rust is a ferric (iron) oxide formed by the chemical combination of the iron with oxygen. Water is a compound of oxygen and most people know that the chemical symbol for water is H_2O. Each water molecule contains two hydrogen atoms and one oxygen atom. The air is a mixture of gases but is mainly composed of 1/5 oxygen and 4/5 nitrogen. Oxygen will pass through thin films of paint either from water on its surface or directly from the atmosphere when no moisture is present. Therefore a chemical inhibitor must be present below the surface coating. A *very thick* surface coating will prevent corrosion, but this is not practicable on a car body except in the case of the underside, where a very heavy coating can be applied.

You can see good cars anywhere, where corrosion is allowed to run wild. The attitude should be to kill wherever it can be seen. This way the life of a car can be indefinitely extended so far as corrosion is concerned.

The interior of body cavities should be protected by injecting one of the special fluids produced for this purpose, such as 'Waxoyl'. Often drilling is not required, the liquid being injected through screw holes from which the screws have been temporarily removed. A pressure type (trigger-operated) oil can is useful for injecting the fluid.

If you remove the carpet you may find access holes plugged or taped over which can be used for injecting the fluid. It is a job to be done thoroughly; therefore treat every cavity you can find, drilling small holes if need be. Pay particular attention to the body channel sections which strengthen the body to enable it to serve also as a chassis. Spring and other suspension mountings, both above and below, are important. The headlamp shells and their fixing areas are very prone to rust.

In the case of door interiors, which have drain holes, it is a good idea to tape over the holes and inject about a pint of fluid. After, say, two hours the tapes can be removed and the excess fluid drained and collected for re-use.

'Waxoyl' will not burn the hands or clothing and can be removed with white spirit (turpentine substitute). It is obtainable from Finigans' Eltringham Works, Prudhoe, Northumberland, England.

'Kurust' contains lead and acid and is harmful to the skin, clothing and eyes; it may be removed with methylated spirits.

The Economics of the Used Car

If you can do most maintenance and repair jobs yourself or know some reliable man who will do the work cheaply, then a used car will provide the cheapest motoring. If a car is looked after properly it will last a very long time indeed. If you can just afford to run a car this is the way to do it, at minimum cost. The newer a car is the greater its depreciation. Depreciation tapers off virtually to nothing after a few years and when you rid yourself of this you have freed yourself from one of the heavy charges of owning a car. A car that is ten years old or more can be in excellent condition and in getting to that age it can give you reliable service and continue to do so almost indefinitely.

It is generally reckoned that the life of a car ends when some repair is required the cost of which is equal to or is greater than the market value of the car. This is not necessarily true if you look at it another way. If you have had the car for a year or two or even longer, it is a known quantity; you know where it is sound and you know where it is weak, or you will do if you are the sort of person we are talking about. We are talking about a car owner who is knowledgeable about cars and who has practical ability and experience or who can obtain assistance cheaply. To others, what we are saying does not apply. If you intend to keep the car for a number of years then the cost of the repair, while it may equal the value of the car, will still be much less than the cost of a new used car, which you would obviously want to be a much later model. Once the repair is done the car could well continue to give good service for several years.

If you do intend to run the same car for a long time, it will pay you to bear this in mind when you buy it. Clearly, over

Fig. 9. This shows a side jacking point. Check as in Fig. 6, but the whole of the underside of the car should be examined. If corrosion is excessive the car will not pass the Department of the Environment test and welding repairs are expensive.

the years many repairs and replacements will be necessary; therefore buy a car that is easy to deal with. Avoid cars where there is inaccessability, cars which have complicated suspension systems, and cars that have had a long run and are likely to come off the production lines. Avoid foreign cars; spares for these are often very expensive and difficult to obtain, particularly in an oldish model.

Finally if you want your car to last a long time with the minimum of trouble learn to drive it properly. Drive it smoothly. Brake gently over a distance rather than harshly over a few feet. If you are alert to what you are doing braking can often be avoided simply by anticipation. Do not hold the clutch pedal down for long periods. You need inconvenience nobody if you bring the gear lever into neutral, keeping your hand on the lever ready to engage 1st gear. Do not use the gears instead of the brakes, this is only justified when descending long hills and on ice; in normal driving it can place heavy stresses on the transmission.

The Car and its Faults: A Summary

Sometimes when a fault is known to exist, there will be some doubt about how serious it is. To put the car right is it a question of £10, £20, £50 ... or what? We have already mentioned various troubles that are likely to arise as the result of misuse or honest wear and tear and we re-state them below and try to give some idea of the repair cost. To give exact figures in a book is impossible; they vary so much between one car and another and are so soon out dated that they would be useless.

The Battery

If you are lucky you may buy a car that has just been fitted with a new battery. You may be told that a new battery has been fitted, but that may have been two years ago. More likely the battery will be on its last legs. It will cost a few pounds. You can expect to have to replace the battery.

The Tyres

Tyres are expensive, if you have to buy four (or five) it is a very important expense. You can easily check current tyre prices.

The Clutch

If the clutch is worn it will be quite expensive to have it put right. The cost of the new parts is not great, but the work required to fit the parts is considerable. It is a major repair. Of course only adjustment may be required; you could probably do this yourself but in any case it would not cost much.

The Brakes

Fitting new brake shoes is the kind of work often done by the car owner. The cost of a complete set of shoes would not be very great, but if they have to be fitted at a garage this would make the job quite expensive. Brake adjustment is quite easy and any car owner should be able to do it.

Electrical Troubles

These can be expensive, depending on what they are. If the battery is not being charged, this could mean a new dynamo or alternator (alternators are considerably more expensive than dynamos), or a new control box. If you can do the work yourself the cost would not be very great, but with garages charges added it would tot up to a fair sum.

The cost of starter repairs would be about the same as for a dynamo, but if a new starter ring has to be fitted to the flywheel this would be an expensive repair.

Faults in the wiring are much more serious. The time involved in putting them right may be considerable and the cost therefore correspondingly high. Faulty light units or bulbs are easily replaced.

On the other hand ignition trouble is usually simple and the owner should be able to do it all himself. Generally all that is needed is contact breaker points adjustment, fitting a new set of plugs or a new rotor. If a new distributor was required this would be an expensive item. Re-wiring the ignition (High Tension system) is not a difficult or expensive task.

Body Corrosion and Damage

All body work is expensive to have done professionally and generally speaking the car owner is not too successful, appearance wise, when he tries his hand at it. Serious corrosion affecting strength of stressed members is a very different matter. It is possible to buy parts for strengthening corroded bodies, but these have to be welded. From the safety point of view these repairs must be done correctly, and the 'Odd Jobber' is a definite risk for this sort of work. Body work of this kind is expensive.

You may be tempted to buy a car that has slight body damage because of the drop in price that must result. Remember, even if there is no misalignment of the wheels so that only appearance is affected, this is not a do-it-yourself job and will be expensive to have put right.

Suspension Trouble

If only new shock absorbers are required some mechanically adept car owners can do the work. Each shock absorber will cost a few pounds. It is quite an expensive repair if a garage has to do it.

Spring trouble is usually expensive. Wear in the front suspension is likely to cost quite a bit to have put right and neither of these jobs can be done by most car owners.

Steering

Slackness in the steering can *sometimes* be put right by adjustment, but usually new ball joints are required. This is not really a do-it-yourself job, and will be fairly expensive to have done professionally.

Engine Knocks

Internal knocks in the engine indicate that a replacement engine is required. It is quite easy to find out the cost of a reconditioned engine – many motoring magazines carry advertisements offering a wide variety of engines, usually involving taking the old engine in part exchange – or you can enquire at a garage dealing with the make concerned. The cost of the engine plus the cost of fitting it would be so big that unless the rest of the car was in good condition it would not be worth it. A major job.

The Gearbox

Again, this is likely to be a major repair. Gearbox trouble is costly and in most cases the cost would be so high that the rest of the car would have to be good to justify it.

Leakage of Oil into the Cooling Water

This is usually due to a faulty cylinder head gasket and many owners can fit a new one of these themselves. The work would take about three hours. If it has to be done professionally it would not be very expensive. However, if the cylinder head was distorted, it would need to be trued and this would materially increase the cost. Worst of all, there might be a crack in the head or cylinder block. Usually there are local firms who will true up the joint face of the cylinder head at reasonable cost, but a cracked cylinder block is a different matter; it means a replacement engine is required.

Misalignment of the Wheels

This would normally be the result of accident damage resulting in distortion of the body. The car is virtually only fit for the scrap heap.

Drive Axle Whine or Knock

This would normally indicate crown wheel and pinion trouble and repairs would be very expensive.

Universal Joints

Universal joints in the drive shafts are usually noisy when the drive reverses, for example when you accelerate and then quickly remove your foot from the accelerator. On front wheel drive cars they also give the 'Knock on Lock' symptom. Replacing the joints is work that some motorists can do themselves. It is not a very expensive repair.

Slack in Front Wheel Bearings

If these bearings are ball bearings, then new bearings must be fitted. Some car owners could do this work themselves. If the wheels have taper roller bearings, these can be adjusted in accordance with the car manufacturer's instructions. Again, this is not a very expensive repair.

66

3

Making Offers – Completing Your Bargain

The test of your assessment of the market value of the car comes now. If you have judged correctly you will be able to buy or sell the car concerned quite quickly, even if it is not to the first buyer who approaches or from the first seller.

But all the care you have taken to hit upon the right price can be lost in seconds if you allow yourself to lose your head at the last minute. Nothing is easier than to say 'oh! well I'll pay the bit more' or 'all right I'll settle for your (lesser) figure'. So stick to your guns for at least the first three or four possible bargains, or you will be throwing away hard cash! If four independent people all insist that your idea of the price is ridiculous, then perhaps you should re-assess and come down (or up if buying) by a little to meet them.

Remember, as we said in an earlier chapter, a car is only worth what someone *will pay* for it. And there has to *be* a someone.

Weak/Strong Concept

Guard against being a weak buyer. That is someone who gets over-determined about a particular car and becomes a fool in a hurry. The seller, if he is any good at judging personality, will recognize your problem and hold out for his top price. That is, if he is a strong seller!

A strong seller is one who does not mind if he does not sell. One who has not allowed his finances to get over-stretched and who can afford to hold on for the next possible purchaser who may be along in a minute.

A buyer's philosophy ought to be that there are plenty more cars down the road as good or better at the real market price. A seller's philosophy should be that if the first buyer won't accept that the price is not too high there will be plenty about who will. Again, if four or more people walk away from a deal (and stay away) he should begin thinking whether he has judged the price a little on the high side.

A strong buyer can learn to recognize a weak seller and a strong seller can spot a weak buyer. Here are a few symptoms to look for.

A strong buyer is ready with the 'lolly' and may even carry enough cash on him. He is quite prepared to return swiftly with the cash once the price is agreed. He is in no hurry and will let his offer stand a day or two, subject to his not finding an alternative car at his price straight away. He does not need more than 'minutes' to arrange finances or to negotiate some H.P. contract. He wants the type of car, but not necessarily your car.

A weak buyer is hesitant about saying where the money is to come from and how soon. But he *must* have the car quickly.

A weak seller cannot get rid quickly enough. He needs the 'lolly' for his new car, or house, or wife, etc. He is well committed on H.P. for the telly, washing machine etc. He may have lost his job. He has probably grudged giving a good car an appropriately good advertisement in the most suitable medium. He mistakenly thinks abbreviated wording will be saving him money.

A strong seller, although there are exceptions, is prepared to spend out on a compelling advertisement and will have made quite sure the car is looking immaculate when you arrive. He will be sticking to his price.

Psychology
It follows from the brief amount already said that there is much psychology involved in the interaction between buyer and seller. Initially this may be on the telephone, but mostly it is likely to be when the two parties meet.

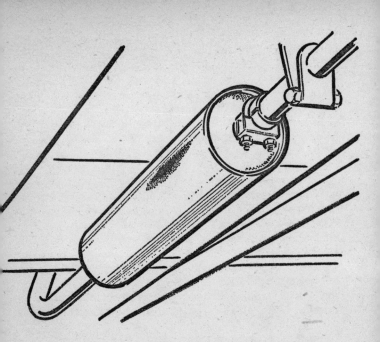

Fig. 10. Check the exhaust system for corrosion or makeshift repair. Renewal of the exhaust system can be expensive.

From the selling point of view the prime essential of any initial phone conversation is to get the person to *come* and see the car. It follows that if he has not seen the car it must be 99 per cent certain he won't buy it. Be prepared before the phone rings with lots of reasons why the car simply *must be seen!* and, *tried!* The psychological advantage normally lies with the person who persuades the other party to put himself out by travelling to ensure that the car be seen. Thus, if as a buyer, you can persuade someone to bring a vehicle *to* you, you are almost certain to be on a winner! He has clearly demonstrated he is desperate to sell. (But watch out for a swindler).

When a person arrives to view his car a strong seller will not allow the meeting to be unduly protracted unless he is sure of a weak buyer, in which case he stands his ground till the buyer comes up to his price. A strong buyer equally, will remain brief and to the point, and will tend to make a swift 'take it or leave it' offer to a weak seller.

If it were not for the weak/strong concept there would never by any disagreement over the price! A buyer would simply come along armed with his knowledge of present day value and his offer based on the condition of the car compared to 'average' (see page 13) would be accepted. His offer would have been reduced to account for foreseeable exceptional repairs or increased a fraction if the car was perfect.

As a shrewd buyer you should decide what to offer in a neutral way, disregarding weakness or strength. Then consider whether the seller is going to be open to offer below that true value price (which may not be the same as the price he was asking) owing to any weakness, and offer accordingly. Thus you face him squarely with reality and cut through any moonbeams he may have gazed along.

Compelling Weaknesses

Often a dealer is open to offers. One compelling reason is finance. A squeeze by the bank or payment for building work going on may require quick drawing in of capital, for example. Purchase of extra stock may have left him a little short. Most manufacturers insist on full payment for new cars *before* they are delivered from the factory, especially in boom conditions. And contracts will have been made to accept certain allocations of new stock. New stock has a nasty habit of being held up by strikes, etc., and then suddenly coming in just when the garage is not ready for it. Large sums have to be found immediately or the allocation may be jeopardized and go to a competitor. Thus there are times when it suits a dealer to get rid. He may have held the car a long while and the cost of keeping it is mounting against it all the time. He would be better off with faster moving stock.

70

A shrewd seller has advertised his price in advance but may have decided he will in fact drop it a little, thus giving an illusion of a bargain to the prospective buyer. Everyone loves to think they have won a little.

If you are selling *to* a dealer (in part exchange or not) you may gamble by not offering to drop the price at all if you feel sure the garage is desperate for stock to sell. Remember they have to have stock to achieve turnover and thus make profits. If they have just opened new showroom space or sales have been running at a high level, they must have replacement stock to survive. There are often times when they just cannot *get* enough of 'em!

A dealer with a large throughput of cars and thus a high quick turnover is likely to be able to pay a little more for your car. This is because, as he will not keep it so long, overhead costs and interest on capital are correspondingly reduced on each car he handles. He makes his profits on the huge turnover at a low level of profit mark up. By keeping selling prices low he attracts more buyers. Conversely the dealer who works on the principle of a high mark up on a smaller number of units is bound to want to pay less for your car. The dealer knows that every car he takes in to stock must earn a certain percentage level of profit for him. Once a car looks as if it is not going to make profitable money he must clear it out at as small a loss as possible in order to take on profitable stock. He knows that unless turnover *is moving* – and the bulk of it *profitably* – he is going to show a thumping loss within a short time. In a *sudden slump* he must slash hundreds of pounds off stock in order not to be left filled with overpriced stock which cannot sell at his prices and unable to buy in fresh stock at the new low level. So the ball is not always in his court!

Salesmanship
We here deal with what to say and not say as you lead up to the point of striking the actual bargain. How to word advertisements, how to spruce up your car before you sell it and other subjects will be discussed in Chapter 7.

If there is something worth saying – say it! What the prospective buyer has *not heard* about your car or does *not know* about the supply demand situation at the moment, etc., will not influence his decision! Excepting lies, all's fair in love and war – and selling cars!

If the car has a scarcity value, mention it. Point out a low mileage but don't mention a high one unless you have to. If the car has extras that you have decided not to keep (see page 114) even though *you* know they are worth little or nothing in the market, you can at least glamorize them all! If expensive mechanical attention has just been completed, explain it and benefit from the fact it has been done. It cost you enough! If the bodywork is unmarked, praise it, praise it! If the buyer has come a long way, remind him!

Conversely beware of agreeing too readily with faults or disadvantages that the buyer is likely to be pointing out. If all cars of the particular model have a design shortcoming you can always say, if the buyer should raise the point as a serious negative one (but no need to mention it otherwise), that 'all these cars are the same and the price takes this into account'. Which it does because your price has been based on market opinion.

When all has been said that can honestly put the greatest appeal on to the car, and reasonable inspection by the buyer has been allowed, it is usually best to make it clear what your final price is and that the buyer must accept it now or leave it. Never promise to keep a car for anyone. It is too easy to miss a sale to a 'real' buyer. This forces him to make the decision before he goes and sees a better car. Even if he does go away for a while if your price is right he is likely to come back anyway, so you haven't much to lose.

Once you have agreed to accept an offer or he agrees to pay your price the cardinal rule is: *Do not part with the car or the log book until you have got the money.*

A cheque (unless it is a banker's guaranteed draft) is no use until your bank have informed you that it has been cleared. If the buyer wants you to, you can arrange for express clearance to speed things up. The buyer *must wait* if he insists on using a cheque. Far quicker and better to deal in cash. My advice for 'doubtful' dealers is the same if you sell to one. Suing for long overdue cash is not a cheap pastime for the private individual. Even 'quality' garages can be pretty sharp and keep you waiting when it comes to paying up. But if they are a public company or they have a franchise for selling a good make of car you are probably safer. Such firms cannot risk a stink in local papers.

A private buyer may be able to arrange instalment purchase for himself through a reputable finance company so

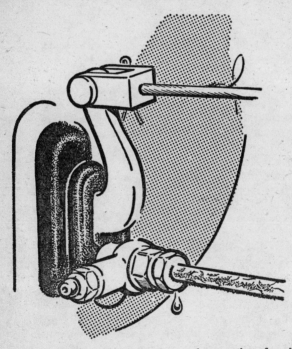

Fig. 11. Check all hydraulic pipes and connections for oil leakage. An extreme case is shown. A darkened area of the covering mud indicates a leakage. Any leakage is a serious fault. Also check the pipes for corrosion.

that although he pays in easy stages you receive your cash immediately. The usual way this works is for him to arrange his loan with the finance company who then pay him the full amount of the loan. He is thus able to give you his personal cheque drawn on his own bank. You will not necessarily know that he is paying over the hurdles.

Refuse to accept payment by instalments yourself unless you want to be a money lender! In any case you could run into serious legal difficulties.

Chapter 5 warns you of other legal requirements and safe-guards for making a sale and should be read carefully.

Buying-manship
You will have gathered that the buyer should be working on the opposite tack to the seller. If you are making a low offer then you should 'make as if to go' and be fully prepared . . . to lose the bargain! The feeling of 'take it or leave it' about your offer to the seller has to be convincing to work. Do not leave an offer standing for more than a specified day or two and do not say you will do this until the offer has been refused outright. There is no point in leaving it open initially as a bargaining point for the seller to take advantage of. Better to force his decision. Have the cash ready if you can. Everyone loves to see the colour of your 'lolly' and its immediacy *is* compelling.

Even more so perhaps than with selling, a convincing argument can influence the price. Spell out every disadvantage you can think of against hanging on to the seller. Point to all the faults you find on the car. Remind him how happy he is going to be when he is rid of it.

Once a deal is decided, just as when you are selling, you need your wits about you. Only part with the cash in return for the car *plus* the log book. If the seller insists that your cheque will have to await clearance, make sure that you have a proper receipt and that you are satisfied the person *is* the true owner of the car.

Chapter 5 is essential reading if you are to safeguard yourself.

Striking the Actual Bargain

At the front of this book and again in the beginning of this chapter we solemnly declared that *the* time for a cool clear head is the moment at which the bargain is struck. Emotional detachment is indispensable.

A good tip is to write down *before* opening your mouth *why* you are about to spend more or accept less than you were bargaining for. Are the reasons valid? Has a well presented argument about this car or this offer persuaded you to overlook the possibility that there may be plenty more cars or buyers available? Is the seller trying to rush you? If he mentions others who are after doing the deal remember that they will have to pay quite a lot more to compete with your 'here and now' offer, or it will not be worth his while taking the risk they will pay the extra. If the buyer is trying to panic you into selling low, why does he want this car so much? How many other equivalents does he *know* exist?

If in doubt; don't panic! Let the other party name his figure for the best 'bargain' he is prepared to accept. He may easily make exactly the mistake you are trying to avoid and throw you the advantage! Anyway you can always refuse, and carefully reflect before making a counter offer.

Some negotiators are inveterate hagglers. They always pitch a figure high to start with as seller, or low as buyer, on the principle that by apparently meeting you a bit with their revised offer you are likely to fall for it being so charitable a gesture. In fact it was their real offer all the time! Some buyers are pathological 'bargain' hunters and will not buy unless they feel they have got something 'off'.

Both the above sorts in my opinion waste a lot of time and increase the difficulty of striking a successful bargain for the two parties. The risk of making a big mistake in the heat of the moment is much greater for the private individual unless he is remarkably quick witted. He may lose several good cars, as a buyer, and, with his unduly low offer, secure a packet of trouble from some dishonest seller. Or in selling he may waste time and money on advertising at such a high price nobody has their appetite whetted sufficiently for them to even come and see his car.

If you must play games of this kind decide your final figure before you kick off!

Far wiser on the whole is to work out what the market is signalling about the true value of the type of car in question, as described in Chapter 1, make allowances for condition, and then stick to your guns. You won't win them all as they say (no-one can do that) but the chances are you will not be disappointed or robbed!

What to do when the car is yours!
It is easy to overlook immediate legal requirements. Is the car taxed and insured? You must have the O.K. from your insurance company before you drive the car away. (See also Chapter 5.)

Has the radiator got anti-freeze (in winter)? Have the tyres been checked recently for pressure, is the engine oil sump full, and the gearbox oil level correct? Is the radiator water topped up? Petrol? When was the battery last looked at?

Whatever you do, drive extra carefully until you are familiar with all the controls.

4

Financing

Important legal aspects of financing are dealt with in the next chapter.

As with buying the car itself, it's easy to be rushed into an expensive agreement if you do not make proper comparisons first.

Cash

Those who can afford to pay cash always come off best for two reasons. One, they can usually strike the best bargain, being 'strong' buyers (see previous chapter), and two, it is extremely unlikely that the money they use has been invested at a higher return than the interest they would have to pay on a borrowing.

Everyone however cannot have spare cash at their fingertips and probably most people depend on having the money from the sale of their old car before they can afford the new one.

Bank Loan

For those who can get one a clearing bank straightforward overdraft is, normally, the cheapest form of loan. The interest charged stops the day *any* repayment is made – on the amount repaid – leaving the interest mounting only on the remaining balance borrowed.

Otherwise, if you cannot borrow free from 'Aunty Jill', the cheapest way to raise the money is likely to be a bank loan at *simple* interest, repayable by instalments. Any good bank manager will normally be agreeable to make such a loan – especially if a large part of it is only tiding over till you have sold the last car – to a customer with a good track record in the handling of his account and a generally sound financial position.

A *simple* interest loan works in the following way. The bank agrees to lend you whatever total sum they are willing to, and you promise to repay within a definite period of time, for example by monthly instalments. You are free to pay back quicker if you prefer, without extra charge. You also save some interest! Interest rates are agreed between you at the start to be so much *over* what is called the 'Base Rate'. For example, if the Base Rate was 8, you might be asked to pay $2\frac{1}{2}$ per cent 'over Base' which means $10\frac{1}{2}$ per cent. If Base Rate moves up to 9 unfortunately you find yourself paying $11\frac{1}{2}$ per cent but sometimes it moves down. The point that matters is how much 'over Base' you have agreed to pay. With a *simple* interest loan of this kind which you are paying off at regular intervals, interest is only charged on the amount *still outstanding* as each reduction is made. Therefore the amount of interest decreases as the capital sum outstanding is reduced. Interest is usually debited at six monthly intervals to the borrower's current account.

Comparing Loan Costs

For purpose of comparison of the cost of borrowing a particular amount the length of time to the end of the contract when the last payment is made must be the same. If someone lends you money over a two year period he naturally expects his money to earn at least twice as much for him as it would during a one year loan). Thus, supposing you wanted to borrow £500 over one year, you should ask each prospective lender how much over £500 this will have cost you by the end, allowing for the *same speed* of repayment.

Compound Interest

Compound interest confuses most would-be borrowers although they know instinctively that it is bad news for their team. 'Easy terms' (a euphemism for hire purchase) and the

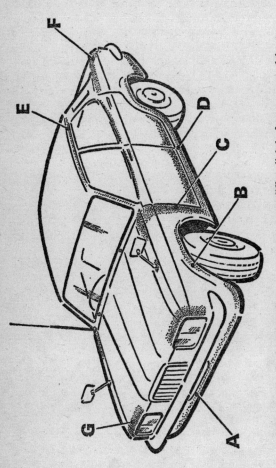

Fig. 12. The body points that are prone to rust differ slightly from one model to another. Likely places are shown: A – along the front; B – wheel arches; C – edges of front body panels; D – sills and door bottoms; E – roof gutters; F – rear wings; G – area round headlamps.

majority of other loans, whatever they may be called, work on the basis of *compound* interest.

Compound interest is calculated like this: you agree to pay a certain rate of interest, for example 12 per cent. This interest begins to be payable from the moment the loan starts and at each charge date the appropriate amount is added to the sum still outstanding during that charge period. On the second and subsequent charge dates interest is still calculated at 12 per cent on the total amount of the loan every time. Thus you find yourself paying a great deal more than you would with a *simple* interest loan.

So you must ask whether the interest you will be paying is to be on a *compound* basis or a *simple* basis. Fortunately there is a convenient formula by which a quoted percentage rate that is to be *compounded* can be converted for comparison from the quoted *simple* interest rate. It is not perfect but is near enough for our purposes. All you do is multiply the quoted rate by 1·8. Thus a quoted rate of 11 per cent *compound* is really equal to a *simple* rate of $11 \times 1·8 = 19·8$ per cent! No wonder people refer to others heavily committed to H.P. as being 'on the drip'!

Since lending money to 'friends' can be so highly dangerous our personal conclusion agrees with that sound adage – 'Neither borrower nor lender be'.

Special Bank Loan

Some banks offer a special type of loan facility which, although it is *compound* and not a basic *simple* interest loan, normally works out rather cheaper than other alternative loans. If you are refused a *simple* interest basis loan it is worth enquiry about this. You are not necessarily affected by changes in the basic rate (which, if interest rates are running high, sometimes even makes it cheaper than the *simple*-interest loan).

Advantages are that in the event of your death no more has to be paid by your estate provided repayments are up to date. (H.P. can usually only be insured like this at extra cost), there is no lien (right to possession) over the car by the

80

bank, and, should you decide to repay the outstanding balance early, the interest charges up to that date are not increased (with H.P. companies they usually are) to compensate the lender for early termination of his fixed rate contract. The bank quotes you a *fixed* rate, a *fixed* amount of interest and a *fixed* monthly repayment figure and this all remains during the term of the loan.

Another point to know about bank loans (not to be mixed up with ordinary overdrafts on current accounts) is that in some countries interest paid above a certain amount is allowable against tax. This may be valuable to a heavy tax-payer since the allowance is usually against the highest rate he pays. The lender is invariably quick to point out if this is possible but one should be careful to check with a good adviser, for example an accountant how such assurances work out in practice.

Borrowing Against Life Assurance

Borrowing against your own life assurance policy can be a good way to raise money and may work out as cheap or cheaper than going to the bank. Again, tax relief may be allowable. Effectively you are borrowing your own money because they will only lend usually according to how much the surrender value of the assurance policy was at the time of the loan!

Personal Loan from a Reputable 'Household Name' Finance Company

As a private seller it is sometimes worth informing a prospective buyer who may not know, that he can often arrange *for himself* a personal loan (the interest on which also may be tax allowable) within a day or two simply by contacting one of the well known finance houses who specialize in selling (they call it 'giving') credit for car purchases. Thus he can buy your car virtually in the same way he might hire purchase one from a dealer and the loan is likely to work out substantially cheaper than H.P. would.

Usually the finance company, provided they have been

able to establish that your creditworthiness is satisfactory, is not concerned with whether you are buying a car or a caravan, or even a stereo set. They are simply selling you a *personal loan* facility. This type of loan, while it costs more than the others so far discussed, is still likely to be a long way cheaper than hire purchase.

It must not be confused with another type of 'personal loan' which can be arranged for you by many garages. The difference between the type of 'personal loan' the garage will help you sign up and an ordinary Hire Purchase Agreement is usually only that, where tax relief is possible, because it is called a 'personal loan', you can save the tax. This makes it just a shade cheaper than straightforward hire purchase. But it is *not* going to be as cheap as the proper *personal loan* discussed at the beginning of this section, which has to be arranged by yourself with the finance company.

Should you wish to make an early settlement of such a *personal loan* from a reputable finance company, for example if you decided to sell the car, they will usually (although there is no legal obligation to do so) waive some of their entitlement to the interest that would have become payable as the loan continued. Naturally they are not over generous about early settlement because they are in the business of medium to long term lending and their rates are calculated to be profitable on loans which extend for their full period. The basis upon which reductions in interest payable upon early settlement are frequently calculated is known as the rule of 78ths. It can be used as a rough guide.

If you add together all the numbers 1 plus 2 plus 3 . . . and so on up to 12 you will find the total is 78. The total interest payable in one year is regarded as being paid off in the proportion of 12/78ths in the first month, 11/78ths in the second and so on, down to one 78th in month 12. When you settle up early you are normally expected, in addition to paying off the outstanding amount on loan, to fork out the proportioned interest that would have been payable during the *next* three months had the loan not terminated. Thus if £X is the amount of interest payable in one year and you decide to settle up after three months you will have to pay the first six portions of interest, which will amount to 57/78ths of £X. (12/78ths plus 11/78ths and so on down as far as 7/78ths).

However should you decide to take out a further loan immediately, for example, to finance your next car, this early termination 'liability' payment can usually be reduced by about half. It depends on the good will sought by the company.

Hire Purchase

I have put this second last in the chapter because, disregarding the prospect of going to some money lender which is dealt with finally, H.P. is the most expensive normal means used to finance buying a car.

Because the garage dealer becomes involved in helping you sign up the contract with the hire purchase company he collects a nice commission. On large amounts this can be very fat indeed and enough for him to make you a better part exchange offer on your old car or perhaps to add a few extras to the one you are buying, euphemistically throwing these goodies in 'free'. The 'personal loan' contract which he may offer to arrange for you and which may save you a little tax as described on page 82, also allows him commission. Sometimes where the salesman collects the commission personally you will find he is keener to sell you the car on H.P. than for cash! – Supposedly the world's best buyer! It is logical because he has then not only sold you the car on which his boss is likely to pay some commission on top of salary, he has also sold you the H.P.

In addition to the commission, which has to come from somewhere, making H.P. more expensive, the quoted rates tend to be a point or so higher than *personal loans* arranged direct with finance companies. To convert the quoted rate so that you can see its true equivalent annual rate it is best to double the figure and subtract one. This is a good rule of thumb. Thus 12 per cent quoted becomes 23 per cent, in reality!

There is another reason why hire purchase should be regarded as your last resort method of obtaining finance. The rates are usually different according to the age of the car to allow for increasing risk. Thus a new car H.P. contract will have a lower rate than a two-year-old one. A three-year-old car on H.P. will find its contract purchasing rate of interest nearly 50 per cent more than the rate on a new car would be. Contrast this with the *personal loan* that you could have arranged direct with a finance company which has the same agreed rate of interest no matter how old the car happens to be!

To settle early on an H.P. contract is easy. You simply ask the Hire Purchase Company for a settlement figure. As with settling *personal loans* early you will find it's an expensive game because you still have to pay for most of the credit even though you don't use it.

Money Lenders

Many people are tempted by money lenders who advertise extended 'unlimited' credit in the most glowing terms – instant cash, without security. Such firms unfortunately have among their number a few who are little short of crooked, but even the honest companies, because of the very high risks involved with this type of lending, have to charge rates which, by any method of comparison must be regarded as exorbitant. I have seen interest rates quoted which were *four* times as expensive in real terms as normal borrowing rates!

Insurance

In a chapter about finance it seems worth adding a word or two on the subject of insurance. Many drivers are ill advised on this subject. When a new type of car is purchased they chase around as many brokers and insurance companies as they can find to get the best quote. Having done so they feel relieved and satisfied with the 'bargain' and the whole subject gets tucked away in a far away recess of the mind till the premium renewal date comes round. When it comes, unless

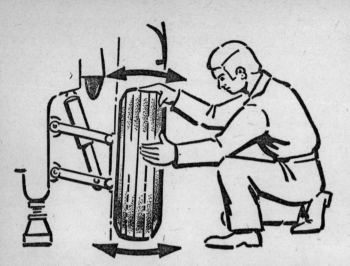

Fig. 13. Check for play by rocking wheels in the vertical direction, as shown. Play denotes king pin (swivels) and/or a wheel bearing slack. Remember, a *trace* of play is essential in taper roller wheel bearings.

the amount to pay has gone wildly up, or they suspect a 'no claims bonus' (it's not a no blaims bonus) should have been increased, they pay up quite cheerfully.

They quite overlook the fact that the present value of the car, which they were insuring to cover, may have reduced considerably! Plenty of cars are still being insured comprehensively when they hit the scrap heap! Also, unless the policy specifically included an arrangement to pay the full 'new' value – which would be most unusual and would cost a lot more anyway – no insurance company ever pays out more than the value at the time in the event of a write off. And it will be a no nonsense rock bottom market value at that! You cannot win with insurance! You will always find yourself paying the full wack and if you are unlucky enough to be on the receiving end, accepting the very least they can get away with paying you.

Third party, fire, theft and full passenger coverage are indispensable. Third party and passenger insurance are a legal requirement in most countries. A person could otherwise have his whole life ruined by huge damages awarded in court. Remember that although a hurt party may wish to forgive they almost always have advisers who, rightly in most cases, show them the folly of so doing. Mercy is not at all appropriate if someone has been disfigured for example and after all that is what insurance is intended to cover.

On the other hand fully comprehensive insurance may not be necessary for all peoples' requirements. Suppose a car originally worth £1,500 is now worth £500. Can you afford to lose £500? Are you accident prone? A few minutes thought on these lines and a comparison of the difference in premium may show up that it is not really worth it to you to continue to insure comprehensively. It depends on your other commitments. While I would in no way advocate a poor man to under-insure I pop the thought in for the richer man who happens to be going to run a cheaper car.

5

Legal Requirements and Swindles

As Seller

You are required to hand over the registration book (and a current Department of the Environment roadworthiness test certificate if applicable) with the car to the buyer, to complete the sale. Chapter 3, page 72 warns you not to part with your car till the money is safely in your hands. Immediately the sale has taken place (if it is in Great Britain) you have to inform the taxation office of the name and address of the buyer to whom the vehicle has been handed over. You can use their special form obtained from any money order post office or notify them by letter, remembering to include details of the Registration Mark (number plate number) and the make and class of vehicle.

Your statutory obligation to tax and insure the car (if it was on a public road) now ceases. So don't forget to cancel your insurance cover. Usually you will be able to substitute your next car on to the same policy by arrangement with your insurer. This simplifies insurance matters for you unless you are intending to shop around for a cheaper insurance quotation. Any 'no-claims bonus' built up can also be transferred to the next car and should you change insurance companies the new one will normally honour the bonus entitlement with a similar rating of their own. A no-claims bonus, incidentally, is built up by virtue of the fact that the policyholder has had a vehicle on the road over a long period without a claim. It does not apply to the driver himself. He can change cars if he wants to, although the premium may be different for the new one when he informs his insurance company, *as he must*, but, if he wants to put *another* car on the road (a second car) it will be regarded as a new vehicle and will not build up a 'no-claims bonus' until it has been on the road claim free for the length of time ruled by the policy.

For your own protection when you sell a car a brief note *signed by the buyer* (which you could have ready for his signature) may save you any trouble should the buyer later become dissatisfied, or worse, try to take you to court. No matter how good you may sincerely *believe* the car is, it can go drastically wrong tomorrow, or it might be involved in an accident with blame being laid upon some mechanical defect. To reduce any risk that you could be held liable here is some wording which, to the best of my belief, will keep you safe.

"I.............(buyer's name)........agree to purchase ......(make)......car bearing the registration mark...... ......from........(your name)..........of........(your address)........and that I have seen tried and tested the car and that the recorded mileage shown on the speedometer/ odometer is........miles. Signed............(buyer's name) ....Address..............Date.........."

Outstanding Hire Purchase Commitment of the Seller
If you bought your car on H.P., it is *illegal* to sell it if any repayments are still outstanding. The debt has to be settled *before* the car leaves your possession.

Legally when a car is bought on H.P. full title of ownership does not pass to the buyer until the H.P. contract is fully paid up at the end of its term (or by early settlement). The garage dealer in law sells the car to the H.P. company and it becomes their property. They in turn hire it to you under the agreed terms of your H.P. contract, and legal ownership does not pass to you until completion. (The dealer gets his money in full from the H.P. company at the time of the sale.)

In practice, because the H.P. debt has to be settled *before* the sale by law, it is not uncommon for a deal to be made between private individuals conjointly, at the offices of the finance company! If the buyer wants to be certain that all lien by the H.P. company over the car has been removed (by settlement of the debt) and the seller is unable to do this till he has the money, it is convenient for everyone for the transaction to be witnessed by the finance company in the privacy of their premises. This way the law can be complied with by the money passing to the H.P. company a few seconds before the 'sale' of the car itself is completed! And all three parties should find themselves amicably contented.

When you have bought your car using a personal loan arranged with a finance house, although it may not be illegal to sell the car before settling the debt, you will probably find that to do so would be in breach of a clause in your contract.

Legal Requirements as Buyer
It follows from what has been said with regard to the seller's responsibilities above that the principles 'let the buyer beware' and 'your eye is your merchant' are likely to be your only consolation should you buy a dud.

Detecting a possible swindle or a forgery of a registration book is discussed on page 96 but it's very hard to protect yourself from an outright swindler after it is too late. They are too slippery! – And they are difficult to track down, but, if they are known criminals, that becomes a police matter. For ordinary protection against a small time dishonest seller who thought he might get away with something you didn't notice before buying, a signed declaration will do no harm and may prove extremely useful. No wording can cover every contingency but the following example should suffice.

"I......(seller's name)......agree to sell (year)........ (make and type).............car bearing registration mark ....to.........(your name)........of......(address) ....and that it is free from all financial lien

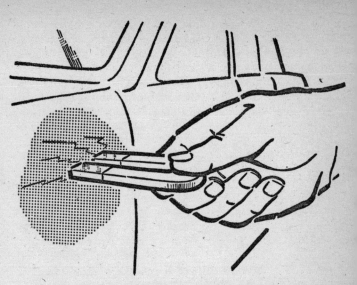

Fig. 14. Check the body with a magnet for 'filled' areas, indicating repair to corrosion or other damage.

and that the recorded mileage shown on the speedometer/odometer is........miles. The registration book of the car *together with a current and valid Department af the Environment roadworthiness test certificate* is handed over with the car to..........(your name)..........*Signed*............
(seller's name)..........Address..........Date........"

The words referring to the roadworthiness certificate italicized above would be ommitted if they did not apply under the law. In Great Britain they would usually be needed on a car over three years of age.

If you are buying from a private individual the signed declaration together with your receipt (which you must obtain) are very important documents to keep. It is simplest if you have a declaration prepared for the seller to sign.

If you buy from a trader you automatically have considerable protection in Great Britain under the Sale of

Goods Act 1893 (and subsequent revisions thereto) which deals with implied terms and items of merchantable quality. You are also protected by the Trade Descriptions Act which, as its name indicates, is legally binding upon a *trader*. You may consider that this additional automatic protection is sufficient for you to dispense with a signed declaration.

However the private individual is not bound by the Trade Descriptions Act and he is difficult to pin down under any other law which makes the signed declaration even more so a wise precaution.

Hire Purchase Obligation Flows with the Goods
Legally, if you bought a car on which repayments were still outstanding unless you could prove that you had been reasonably prudent about satisfying yourself that nothing was owing, you could find yourself liable to pay off the H.P.! Hence the importance of the words 'free from all financial lien' on the suggested wording to be signed by the seller. The hire purchase laws passed in 1965 and the law relating to Factors (traders) afford you some protection provided you took all reasonable steps to establish that no liabilities existed before you purchased.

Under the Factors Law you are entitled to assume that a motor trader who offers a car for sale holds title (is the legal owner) to sell that car. In practice this can mean that he only holds consent of the real owner to pass title. The law covers this contingency which is useful where, for example, a member of the public asks a garage to put his car on show and sell it for him on a commission basis. Theoretically, even if the garage has been cheated, you, as the final buyer should not be sucked in to any legal proceedings. But this particular protection does not apply to a private purchase, which is nearly always a riskier business. (See page 102.)

Nearly all motor traders in Great Britain subscribe to Hire Purchase Information Ltd. where, with a quick phone call, they can check whether credit is outstanding on any car simply by quoting the make and its registration mark. The information is collected from all the finance companies on to

91

one central register. The system provides mutually beneficial protection for all concerned. But the private buyer can obtain access to this method of checking without having to be a paid subscriber. This is arranged free of charge through the Citizen's Advice Bureaux and all you have to do is to ask them to have the car checked upon for you. Alternatively, if you are a member, the A.A. or R.A.C. will obtain the advice for you. The company itself does not deal directly with the public.

Proof of Ownership

Your receipt for your payment for the car, which has been mentioned as being of vital importance, will be your proof of ownership which may be needed when you re-sell. In the case of a car bought from a *trader* you would obtain a re-ceipted sales invoice.

A registration book is *not* a document of title nor proof of legal ownership as a note on it warns you. The person in whose name the vehicle is registered may or *may not* be the legal owner. The name in the book is only that of the person registered with the taxation authority as the *keeper* of the vehicle.

Registering Yourself as the New Owner

So that the registration can be transferred to your name the law requires you to fill your name in on the next vacant space in the registration book and send it immediately to the taxation authority so that they can complete their records. If the car needs to be re-taxed, you do so at the same time. If you do *not* intend to use the car on public roads (parking in the street would be deemed 'using'; the car would have to be kept at private premises, off the highway) you have to inform the authority of this, but you do not need to send in the registration book. Should the car be going to be scrapped (perhaps for spares) or if you will be exporting the car permanently, you have to write this information on the registration book and return it to the authority.

Insurance

Your insurance must by law cover the car from the moment you take possession and drive the car. Your insurance agent/broker or company will give you guidance but the arrangements must have been made in advance and, essentially this means that you *must have either* (a) a cover note commencing from the day you take possession at a time prior to when you collect the car or (b) a blanket 'any vehicle belonging to the policyholder' certificate of insurance on which the company has agreed that the particular car in question will be insured from the said time and date or (c) a certificate of insurance specific to the car and the driver(s) who will drive it valid from just before possession takes place.

Where a new insurance policy is concerned you usually have to start with a 28/30 day 'cover note' until the proper certificate has been prepared. It is essential in our view, in these days of awful inefficiency, for you to keep a note in your diary to see that the certificate comes through on time or that another cover note is issued. Where a policy has been in existence covering your former car which has just been sold and the new one is being substituted on to that policy you usually have to fill out a 'substitution' form so that the policy and/or certificate can be endorsed with particulars of the new acquisition – again, all this must be sorted out in advance. An insurance company will usually be able to cover both cars for a brief period if you have not been able to sell your former car before taking over the new one. Do make sure you have told them exactly what is happening and that you have their acknowledgement that they have received your instructions.

A telephone acknowledgement may be sufficient where a reliable insurance company is concerned for the first few days till the proper papers have had time to reach you. However I would tend to be very careful about this making sure you have an independent witness to the 'phone conversation' and that the person confirming your cover is acting in a *bona fide* capacity for the company. It is much more satisfactory to have everything properly in writing before you step into the driving seat for your own piece of mind, although it is fair to say that no major British insurance company is likely to default over a technicality such as this should you chance to be unlucky and have an accident before written confirmation arrived. The trouble would be if the individual who confirmed the cover to you were to die or some other extraordinary coincidence occurred whereby no-one else in the company knew of the transaction.

Department of Environment Roadworthiness Test Certificate

If the car you have bought is old enough to require one *make sure you get it* and it is a good plan to make a note in your diary when it will have to be renewed, allowing time for any repairs to be done.

Hire Purchase Cooling-off Period

To protect the public from being rushed into H.P. contracts by doorstep salesman of all types and shades of ability to persuade people against their better judgement (and not only in the car business), which, on reflection, those persons realize they cannot afford, a cooling-off period is allowed under the hire purchase laws.

The safeguard only applies to contracts signed *off a trader's premises,* for example if the dealer brought the car round to your house and asked you to sign up there. A special type of agreement has to be used for such a deal, known as a pause agreement. This has to contain a clause which extends you the right to a cooling-off period. You can insist on a pause agreement when you sign up at the garage but in the normal course of events they are *not* used. The law reasons that if you have approached the trader voluntarily and you sign on, you must have had the intention to buy before you went. Whereas if the dealer arrived on your doorstep he might have 'bounced' you into buying in a moment of weakness when you were off your guard. That is

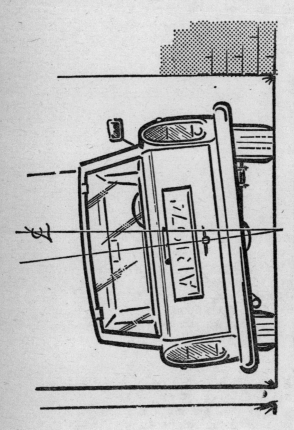

Fig. 15. Check for weak suspension springs. The car should be level (or nearly so) when on level ground. The wall may help by providing a true vertical.

why the protection does not have the force of law in a deal made and signed *on* the trader's premises.

So if you feel you want to have a pause type of agreement, make sure that is what you are being asked to sign. The purpose of the law is to give you more time to reconsider finally whether you *can afford* to pay and you do *want* to pay whatever the instalments amount to at the regular dates defined in the contract. If, on re-thinking your budget, you realize you will not be able to do so you have the right to revoke (cancel) the contract and back out of buying the car provided you do so within the specified cooling-off period. The normal procedure is that you are given one copy of the documents at the time of signing and another copy goes to the finance company. When they accept you as a customer (they have to check on your creditworthiness first) they then have to send you another copy within seven days of accepting the contract. You then have four more days from the day you receive the second copy during which you may revoke the contract, after which, if you have not cancelled, it becomes final and binding. Technically the finance company are under no obligation to avoid delay in letting you have their acceptance (they are only obliged to send you the second copy contract within seven days of the acceptance) but in practice they are pretty quick because otherwise they might lose the business anyway!

Incidentally the idea of pause agreements is not to allow you to take a car on trial for the length of the cooling off period and usually no garage will fall for letting you have the car until after the specified time is up!

Swindles
If anything about a car or the seller seems suspicious to you and is not satisfactorily explained the best advice is to forget that the car ever existed (much as you may have liked it!) and look for something else.

Various simple checks are explained below, the combination of which will usually uncover any tricky dealing. Rogues nearly always forget a detail somewhere along the

96

line and although it might be inadvisable to make any accusations you have the alternative of turning down the chance to buy that car.

Registration Book Details

Check that the vehicle and/or chassis number in the registration book is identical to the number shown on the vehicle manufacturer's patent plate. Also that the engine number accords with that shown in the registration book exactly. See that the colour named in the book is the same as that of the car. Also see that the registration mark (number plate number) is correct.

If the registration mark includes a coding indicating the year of manufacture – had the manufacturer introduced this particular model during that year? Or, alternatively, had production ceased well before that time?

If a new engine has been fitted during the life of the car the fact should have been recorded in the registration book, just as when a change of colour has taken place. If any material item on a car affecting the detailed particulars recorded in the registration book has been altered the law provides that the taxation authority be informed at once, so that the book can be amended accordingly. *It is easy to overlook this when you have work done yourself!*

If your checks show up a different engine number the seller may be able to supply evidence of what has happened in the form of his invoice/receipt from the garage where the work was done. Usually the supplier of the new engine will have included the correct number of the new engine on his invoice and he may even have recorded the mileage of the car when the work was carried out. So if there is an invoice which tallies, even though the owner may not have known to have the registration book brought up to date, you can probably rest assured all is O.K.

There should not be any alterations on a registration book, so suspect any crossings out, or splodges where the numbers or letters are written.

It is quite common for a buyer to phone up previous

owners recorded in the registration book to tally mileages etc. Often people are delighted to help but you must be prepared for a 'flea in the ear' from some!

Service Voucher Book Details and Maintenance Invoices
Nearly all car manufacturers run a maintenance voucher book system. Identification particulars are recorded in it at the time of first sale and, as and when services are carried out at the due intervals, each voucher should have been rubber stamped by the garage doing the work together with a signature and the date. If the identification details are all in order and the stamped vouchers show regular attention with the mileages of the most recent work tallying approximately with that recorded on the speedometer/odometer now, you are provided with a useful additional check as to whether the seller's claims are exaggerated or fair. However, as often as not, the voucher book has long since disappeared whenever less meticulous owners or older cars are concerned.

Most good service garages have the recorded mileage at which a service or repair has been carried out on their invoice, often in a special space printed thereon. If a seller can show you these you can learn a tremendous amount about the car apart from noting that everything tallies as it should with regard to mileage, etc. However, it is rare to find an owner who has kept everything neatly filed ready for the day of sale! The absence of such evidence does not really prove anything.

Confirming true age and mileage by intelligent inspection of condition. (See Chapter 2.)

Department of Environment Roadworthiness Test Certificate
The mileage at which the test was carried out is recorded thereon and should not have been altered. If the speedometer/odometer has been wound back illegally this point is frequently overlooked by the rogue concerned! Sometimes

several years' of certificates are available and the whole sequence can be checked.

Rebuilt Cars which Have Been Write-offs

Dangerous though it is to be too dogmatic, it is our opinion that *any* rebuilt written-off car is not worth buying, no matter how cheap. So if it is a rebuild our advice is – forget it! To check for a suspect rebuild, see chapter 2, page 38.

Stolen Cars

We are grateful for the co-operation of New Scotland Yard in preparing these extra hints which should ensure that you do not find out too late that you have bought a stolen car – a 'ringer'. Remember that a stolen car might well be unroadworthy and, once it has been traced, you may find you have to return it to its rightful owner without any compensation. In law the theft is on you!

The first thing to suspect would be a price that was ridiculously low. Any unusually low price can be suspect unless there is a valid reason for it. Look out for the seller who has no fixed address, who agrees to meet you somewhere at a set time, or who would rather come round with the car to your home. Beware of the seller who can only be phoned at a given time; it may just be a call box. New-looking number plates on an old car would give rise to suspicion.

Pay for the car by crossed cheque so that the person can only get the money by paying it through their own bank account. The safest way to cross the cheque is by writing 'A/C . . [name of person] . . . only' across it at an oblique angle between two lines. The fact that such a cheque has to go through an account should give at least some chance of tracking down the rogue!

If you have a good idea the seller is up to no good see if he will come back again after you have had time to think about the deal. This will give you time to contact the last owner in the registration book and see that he agrees with the story of the car which you have been told. Should he tell

99

Fig. 16. Check that the recorded mileage tallies with the mileage given on the D.O.E. certificate or on recent service and repair invoices. The oil warning light (B) or (C) should go out *immediately* the engine starts, or even when the engine is being turned by the starter (see page 43). An oil pressure gauge (A) should show a normal pressure for the engine (as laid down by the manufacturer) when it is hot.

you the car was scrapped or something quite out of line with the seller's patter, the time has come to call the police.

The police can pin down the date of manufacture of a car

using methods by which the tiniest component may provide the clue.

Recourse under civil law when things go wrong or you feel you have been deliberately cheated

In dealing with a trader you have in Great Britain the protection of the Trade Descriptions Act 1968. This makes it a criminal offence for a false description to be applied to goods during the course of *trade*. As its name implies, it only impinges on traders and does not concern itself with private deals. The Act also appears to apply to anyone who in the course of *trade* talks you out of your car for a ridiculously cheap price by falsely describing its condition to convince you.

If you believe you have been misled by a trader you should discuss the matter with the council weights and measures inspector. He will prosecute the trader if the authority consider the description was illegal. However this does not secure the return of your money by itself. What happens is, if the prosecution proves successful, you then have to take a civil action to obtain the cash. But in practice none of this need happen. The threat implied by the appearance of the weights and measures inspector alone forces the trader to reach agreement with you.

Under the Sale of Goods Act 1893 and subsequent amendments to the act there are, in the eyes of the law, attached to any sale, what are called the 'implied terms'. Principally these are, (*a*) that the seller holds full title to the goods and thus has the right to sell them – no debt is owed against the goods giving prior title to a third person, (*b*) that any description used is accurate – in effect the goods must be exactly as described with no substantial variation, (*c*) that in a case where a sale is made during the course of business (of the seller) whether this business relates to the motor trade or not, the car must be of merchantable quality.

Thus in a private deal (*a*) and (*b*) above assume importance, and if you buy from a motor trader or from someone who is selling the car on behalf of his business, (*a*), (*b*) and

101

(c) are implied. (Note the implications for anyone who is selling in the course of any type of business.)

To be of 'merchantable quality' the car must be suited to the use which any reasonable person would expect of that type of vehicle. For example it might be reasonable to suppose that a car which was described as an *estate* car had an additional load carrying capacity by comparison with its saloon counterpart. But if the word *estate* had *not* been used in the description a buyer might find it very difficult to prove he had been misled. If the seller commends the car for a particular use, or the buyer has *told* him what he wants it for, and the car turns out unfit to do the job, the seller may be held liable. His only let out might be, if he had known the car did not match up to the standard of merchantable quality, if he had made quite certain (probably in writing) that the buyer knew all about whatever was defective. In this regard, because of faults about which he may not know, a prudent business seller will ensure that the buyer gives the car a thorough all round inspection and test run so that it could if necessary be claimed that the buyer's 'eye was his merchant' and that he could have been reasonably expected to discover whatever faults there were during the course of his looking over and trying the car.

Private Sale Prices

It follows from what has been said in this chapter and elsewhere that the risks of purchasing privately are greater than in buying from the trade. The chances of fraud or a swindle are higher and no guarantee goes with the car, or much opportunity for redress should it prove not to be of merchantable quality. Because of the larger element of risk it would seem reasonable to assume that the same car bought privately ought to be a little cheaper than if you were buying it from a dealer. The seller should appreciate this but rarely does! Prices paid tend to be ridiculously close to those the trade would ask. However you may be able to persuade a seller that, despite supply and demand, it is logical for the price to be a bit less!

102

6

Auctions

The advantages of a quick sale and immediate safe cash
appeal to quite a number of sellers, particularly business
people who have to protect their 'cash flow' and keep
company finances sound. It can be a cheap place to look for
the buyer. Be prepared (and have the ability) to keep cool
during the excitement so that you *do* lose a few nice cars if
necessary, when the auction goes above your price. The auction functions as a fast clearing house for huge numbers of
cars, both *wanted* and *unwanted*. Frequently cars are trans-
ported from all over the country so as to be put in the most
favourable auction. Buyers come from all parts if they
happen to be searching for a certain type of car. But it's
a tough game, not for the weak or neurotic, and it's all
cash.

Buying at an Auction
Most of the cars going through an auction are bought by
motor traders at prices which are low enough for them to
add a profit and place the car elsewhere or sell it retail.
Therefore the private individual can hope to put in a winning bid at or just a little above what the trade will pay. This
figure, if his arithmetic has been sound, is likely to be substantially less than he would expect to pay had he bought the
same car from a garage or privately.

Against the saving is the risk of buying a rogue car and
the fact that there is unlikely to be a good warranty such as
there might be if you were purchasing from a reputable
dealer. Your only redress might be if the auctioneer's description (which is usually based on the owner's description

and perhaps an engineer's report) did not include an accurate description of some major defect(s).

Best Auction 'Buys'
If you have decided that you require a second-hand example of a car which has been a very popular model the auction will be a good place to look. This is because of supply and demand. You are likely to find the market is comparatively flooded with such models and that, because they are so easy to come by, the trade regard them as hard to sell. (With a plentiful supply competition becomes much fiercer.) Thus there will be lots of choice and prices are going to be relatively low. All you must make sure is that you only bid on the *good* examples until you get one.

With more unusual cars a lot depends on luck and how many people turn up looking for that sort of car. If a specialist dealer in that model happens to be present he may be able to bid higher than you were anticipating. Nevertheless, throughout the whole spectrum of types, there are bargains to be found.

Rhyme and reason regarding prices on a particular day are sometimes impossible to fathom out. Prices can shoot way above normal levels or they can appear somewhat depressed. Traders themselves are the first to admit that they do not always understand why a particular car came to be knocked down for an extraordinarily high or low price.

Timing
It is worth bearing in mind that if there are twenty or thirty cars of one type going through on a certain day it may turn out that the last few reach lower prices because many of the possible bidders have already spent their money earlier.

But the early bird may secure the car he wants *before* the late bird arrives. The lunch period may prove a good time while a percentage of possible buyers are off the floor. You must decide for yourself how to gamble on timing and the above thoughts are only a guide.

Like any money-making activity, winning at auctions is

hard work. Look at it this way. You may save the equivalent of a week's, or several weeks' wages if luck and your judgement come right. Therefore it is surely worth spending at least one or two days at auctions to get the feel of the game. Talk to a few people and learn what you can. People are usually flattered to be asked and delighted to help.

A car auction is a colourful exciting scene in which there is a rush of activity. You must not allow your judgement to be affected by this general euphoria. An expert auctioneer may talk so quickly that you need half an hour to tune in and follow what he is saying!

Planning
You need time to walk around and inspect all the cars of the type you want and make a note of their lot numbers. It will be useful to watch a few *exactly* similar ones go through to find out prices being reached. Thus you will be able to calculate what your top bid for one is to be. Remember you may have to pay a little more than the regular trade would in order to outbid them. If you cannot establish prices in this way, as on an unusual model, you should be able to work it out from the ways described in Chapter 1 and allowing for dealer's normal profit. (See page 19.)

If you base your price assessments on a good example of the type with an average mileage (see page 23) there is a useful rule of thumb by which you can arrive at the right price for a high mileage or tatty example. Deduct from the price of a good one the cost of obvious expenditure (look at the engineer's report if there is one) required to body and mechanics, tyres, etc., plus £5.00 per 1,000 miles *over* average mileage. *At the right price* such a car can still be good value. But *you* will have the trouble of arranging necessary repairs. With the large savings that can be involved it is worth considering buying a dowdy looking car on the basis that with the money you have got in hand you will be able to afford a respray. If a car has lived in the open unpolished all its life it can look dreadful but still be a very sound buy if you look at it this way.

You must however be careful about condition. Because of limited time you have to take a shrewd and quick guess at condition but, with the help of Chapter 2 and your common sense and experience you should be able to short-list better risks and rule out real duds.

Whether you decide to buy in an auction must depend on your own confidence about your will-power to resist bidding higher than you wanted to. If you doubt your own strength of will then as we said at the start of this chapter, forget it. Remember that the trade can detect what they term a 'retail punter' at once. You are a new face so you stand out anyway. Traders watch to see who takes an interest in their car and once they have noticed you 'falling in love with it' will do their best to pump the price up as far as they dare by bidding against you. Two or three may work together and at the last second melt out of the bidding leaving you with the car at the top price. These men are trained to judge people and they *are* brilliant at it. A tell-tale expression on your face which they noticed by looking at your reflection on a next-door car window may have been all they needed to sum up your eagerness. You would probably be unaware that they had even been observing you! Your only safeguard in this game is therefore your own resolve.

So You've Bought It!

Immediately a car is 'knocked down' to you it is usual for the auctioneers to require a *cash* deposit plus your cheque for the balance. When you will be allowed to collect the car will depend on the rulings by which the company concerned conduct their business. It may be quicker to pay all cash. The process will be quick anyway.

Make sure you receive all the right documents and that you are legally correct to drive away. *See Chapter 3, page 76 and Chapter 5.)*

It is essential that you test the car as immediately as possible once it becomes yours. Any delay may prejudice your right to your money back. Study the auctioneer's conditions of business carefully to see how you stand about this.

Selling at An Auction

Why sell through an auction? Apart from the reasons given earlier many private owners look at things this way: if they buy their next car without involving any part exchange they know that they will be able to get a nice lump off the price. On a new car, perhaps it will amount to 10 per cent off the normal price. Rather than do a part exchange, because they realize that the part exchange price, (or the price they might reasonably expect to sell for ordinarily) may not be more than the price that a trader is likely to pay at an auction by nearly as much as that discount amounts to, they look for gain by selling in the auction and accepting the discount, pocketing the difference.

All they have to make sure is that they put the right reserve price on the car (see later how to pitch your reserve price and why, page 108) and that this realized price (less auctioneer's commission) combined with the discount being given on their next car will work out to the most advantageous deal.

Preparation

Prepare your car meticulously. Attend the auction if possible so that you can give her a last minute dust over should she be spotted with rain marks from standing outside. (If your paintwork is poor, leave the recent rain spots; they mask the scratch marks). You will almost always find that the car has to arrive on the auctioneer's premises at least a day before, so find out the rules. If you can persuade the organizers to put the car through at a good time of day or in a batch where it is not the last of several identical ones it should be to your advantage. The difficulty is that everyone else has got the same idea!

Entering Your Car

Take the registration book and Department of the Environment test certificate (if applicable) with you (in the U.K. – similar documents in other countries) as you will have to give these to the auctioneer together with one of his entry forms filled out.

There will be an entry fee and perhaps a small service charge to pay and the auctioneer's commission will be deducted from the money you receive.

In filling out the entry form you *must* for your own protection be accurate about stating *all* mechanical defects known to you. You must also *state* (unless it is not) that it is a private sale. Otherwise the buyer may have enhanced redress against you should he be displeased, and the transaction may fall within some of the terms of the Sale of Goods Act which it need not have done.

Since it is illegal to sell a car upon which hire purchase is still outstanding you must either:

(*a*) settle the amount owing yourself first or,

(*b*) arrange for the auctioneer to settle for you. He then pays you the difference. (He makes sure the car is not sold for less than the amount he is going to settle for you!)

The entry form is likely to require you to state the *recorded* mileage. Make sure the word *recorded* is included as explained in Chapter 7, page 120. Do not guarantee the mileage unless you have been the sole owner and you know it is correct. Liability for any inaccuracy could fall on you even if it was an earlier owner who cheated.

A preamble to your descriptive wording which to the best of our knowledge should keep you protected should be included in this sort of way: 'to be sold as seen and approved upon buyer's examination and with the following known defects . . .'

Just as you would mention important extras in an advertisement (see Chapter 7), add them to the details on the form. Mention if the car is taxed as the trader tends to be a little more favourable to a car which is ready to sell and which his customer will not need to re-tax for a while.

Reserve Prices

Lastly your reserve price or the minimum you will accept,

108

should be carefully pitched and entered on the form. Except on very old or cheap cars you will be wise to have a reserve price, even though it is not in the auctioneer's interest to damage his reputation by allowing your car to be 'given' away.

You will want to bear in mind the auctioneer's commission which is going to be deducted. But even so you still have to set a reserve either at, or just a little below, what the traders are likely to pay. Otherwise the bidding will not reach your price and no sale will result. Some auctioneers will then phone you at once and say 'Your car did not reach its reserve price; would you prefer to accept the highest bid of £... or have no sale?' KEEP YOUR WITS ABOUT YOU! You can throw your car away if you lose your resolve now! You *can* say 'no sale', and you have only lost your entry costs.

At some auctions special rules apply about reserve prices and you should find out by talking to the auctioneer. For example a reserve price may be invalidated by the style of your car description or its price level. But usually an auctioneer can accommodate what you want if he wants to. Find out or go to a different auction.

Why the necessity for a reserve price? You know (or at least think you know!) you can sell the car yourself elsewhere for that price or a bit more. There is the chance that if there are only one or two bidders, they can, if in league, stop bidding against each other at a low level. They agree between themselves who gets your car afterwards and the one who has it will probably do a similar deal in return to help his friend on another day. But you lose!

Once the auction is over you will receive your money within a few days, usually almost by return of post.

7

Tips When You are Selling

Sprucing up

The majority of buyers are unable to judge the true mechanical condition of a car and have to work on instinct and what it looks like. This is why Chapter 2 is so important to you as a buyer and I hope it will help.

The condition of the body work, however, is critical when you hope to fetch the best sale price (and who doesn't). To illustrate my point I hope you will pardon my telling a true story which shows the disdain one typical motor trader in the west end of London has for mechanical condition. We had an estate car which drank oil in the engine from the day it was new. No one seemed to be able to cure it. After a year and a half of one bill after another my Father finally despaired and decided the car had to go and a new one was duly ordered. By the time it arrived the old one, which had not covered more than average mileage, was using a pint of oil in every ten miles! On the journey to the garage which bought it, of less than an hour, two pints went in.

We arrived and the proprietor looked over the car while my Father explained about the oil, and bent over backwards to convince him the engine was finished. At that particular time new engines were known to be in a very short supply. The man started the engine and switched off again no sooner than it had fired. 'The engine is perfect,' he said, 'but I will have to take a few pounds off for the dent in the rear door and this scratch along the left sill. Mr. Topper, it's a deal!'

Knowing that most potential buyers are going to be persuaded almost entirely by looks it pays real dividends to spend a big effort making the car 'immaculate'.

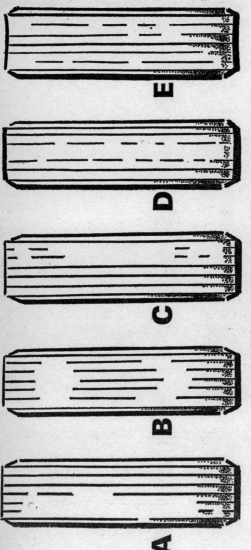

Fig. 17. Tyre wear patterns A, B, and C show the effects of wear due to slack wheel bearings and/or suspension and steering linkage. Misalignment of the wheels will also produce uneven tyre wear. Sometimes the tread is deeply hollowed or 'cupped' in places. D shows a tread with worn centre and sound shoulders, due to overinflation. E shows a tread with sound centre and worn shoulders, due to underinflation. These latter two faults are due to poor tyre maintenance and not to any fault in the car.

Use science. There are some remarkable haze removers on the market to shift traffic grime from paintwork. Take a tip from the motor trade. They always use them. After the stains and dirt are off apply a liberal coat of best polish, or two coats will do no harm! Shine up all the glassware, headlights, all windows, mirrors. Sparkling windows make a world of difference to appearance. Rusty chrome can be polished up with a good proprietary cleaner but if it is beyond this stage a washing-up scouring pad can have a magic effect. If the chrome is nearly finished anyway, you will not do much harm.

Make sure the luggage boot is spotless, like your dining room table. Under the bonnet a few minutes can be well spent. A tin of solvent with which to wash away oil and dirt using a stiff brush can be bought cheaply and the results will be excellent. A more expensive way but which has miraculous results is to ask your garage to steam clean the engine. They have a special machine with parafin and hot water coming out of a powerful jet which will dislodge all the muck from every nook and cranny. You will hardly believe your eyes.

It is important for the battery to have that 'well cared for' look. Make sure it is clean and that any traces of corrosion at the terminals are cleaned off. The terminals should be smeared with vaseline (petroleum) jelly and replaced securely. The distilled water should be topped up to the correct level, just above the separator plates.

Make sure engine oil, gearbox oil, and radiator water levels are all up to their marks. The windscreen washer reservoir should be full and the tyres pressures correct. Any of these small items is easily forgotten. Inside the car the appearance of the dashboard should be impressive. Polish the glass fronts of all the dials. Clean out ashtrays and gloveboxes. (The buyer may be a non smoker and hate the smell of stale ash.) Wipe clean and polish up all interior shiny parts of trim. For example, you may be surprised how many spots of dirt accumulate on the steering wheel bars and how good it looks with a minute or two of attention.

Just as paintwork can have its appearance completely altered with a scientific cleaner you will find that car seats can be transformed in a few minutes, along with door panels and the like. An accessory shop will advise you which is safe to use and the best brand to buy. Or you may prefer to make careful use of a suitable household cleanser at less expense. Carpets should be removed, beaten and then hoovered. For drastic cases try a carpet cleaner too.

Lastly do not forget the head lining. Apart from cloth linings which are rare and usually subject to special cleaning instructions in the maker's handbook, these are best attacked with the same cleaner used on the seats. There are a few upholstery materials used which the makers warn will not stand up to powerful modern cleaners and you should study the car handbook if in doubt. However, if a diluted solution is tried first in an out of the way place you can usually judge for yourself if the risk is worth it.

Rusty body work showing through should be attended to as discussed in Chapter 2. But it is better to do nothing than a bodge job. Such work has a habit of being obvious and is basically dishonest. If a buyer discovers even one smattering of evidence of covering up he won't trust anything else you say about the car.

Because costs are so prohibitive except perhaps for a dealer with facilities, a complete re-spray is rarely worthwhile for a private seller. If you want to have it done always stick to the original colour (if your aim is maximum benefit when you come to sell) and have the work done six months or a year ahead of when you come to sell. This way *you* will have the pleasure of the new look. Whether this merits the high cost is up to you. The better looks will not increase the value of the car by as much as you have had to pay.

Remember as a private individual it is not really your job to point out all the faults of the car. Rather it is the buyer's task to discover them. Only mention a fault if you feel it is only fair to do so. The less you *know* about mechanical faults, an unusual noise for example, the less you can say! However, if a fault is clearly destined to be noticed by every prospective buyer, why not mention it first? The fact you have done so will establish confidence in your buyer and any plus points you mention are thereby enhanced in effect. The position may be different if you are selling a car in your capacity as a businessman. (See Chapter 5 page 102).

Unless a mechanical fault renders the car undriveable or *unroadworthy*, it doesn't always pay to have it mended. Human nature makes the prospective buyer tend to under-estimate what it will cost to put right and in any case (*a*) he may not notice the fault or (*b*) he may not attach the same importance as you might to having such a fault attended to. To sell a car knowing it was unsafe, however, would put you in a dangerous legal position unless you obtained a state-ment from the buyer that he had been informed by you that the fault existed. The details could be tacked on to the buyer's declaration note suggested on page 88.

Accessories

In Chapter 1 we mentioned that 'extras' are worth nothing when you come to sell. All that can be said charitably about them is that if two identical models are on offer side by side, the one with a substantial number of sensible accessories may sell a little easier if the other has none.

Therefore remove your own goodies. Do not leave any live wires. The old wires can be left in position to avoid disturbing trim but they *must* be detached from the power source point to eliminate fire risk and the ends tied out of harm's way. Holes through the body should be treated at the edge with rust inhibitor and a coat of paint, and a grommet of rubber or plastic of the correct size fitted. Nothing looks worse or is more likely to dampen a buyer's enthusiasm than untidy evidence of some fittings having been wrenched off.

Advertising

In the course of assessing the right market price as discussed in the first chapter you will have discovered which is the most appropriate place to advertise. You should also have

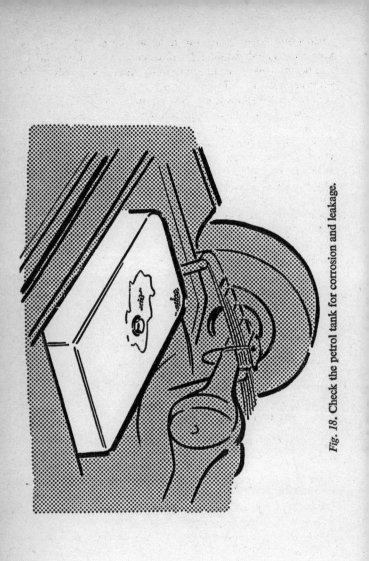

Fig. 18. Check the petrol tank for corrosion and leakage.

learned a lot about making your wording compelling by seeing the experts at work. Which ads. impressed the most? Assuming you have decided to sell privately (see page 19 – is it worth your while?) then here is a check list of *essential* wording:

1. Make	e.g. Marina
2. Model/type	GT or Estate, Mark I, Mark IV etc.
3. Year of first registration	19..
4. Price	£
5. Your 'phone number	043–689–1161 (Sussex), evenings 2240

Any one of the above basic facts omitted renders your advertisement almost useless, which is why we have put them in the form of a checklist. However it is the embellishments to the basic facts which are likely to *sell* your car.

Most advertisement columns allow you to use some bold type to distinguish your ad. from the rest. The important thing to arrest the reader glancing swiftly down the column will, definitely, be the name and type of the car. If the ads. are grouped under the manufacturer's names (e.g. Ford) the type alone may be sufficient. Let the wise-crackers use funny headings. You want to make certain the maximum number of people interested in your type of car *know* that yours is on sale. They are going to be looking through that classification so you must be sure your ad. is right there, looking confident! If the amount of bold type allows, extend it to include the year. This is usually possible.

It is vital to get item 5, your contact point, right. The slightest difficulty in getting hold of you, even an engaged signal tone on the telephone perhaps, can mean that you lose a prospective customer to someone else. Include your dialling code or the name of the exchange. Be on '24 hour' call if you possibly can by giving day and night numbers. If that is impossible give definite times. People normally phone up at sensible hours but remember if they cannot answer your ad. they will be after another one. Every *other* car they may agree to go and view is a 'nail in the coffin' as far as your chance of selling yours is concerned. Few people have the patience to trail round looking at more than a couple of possible cars. That is why under psychology on page 69 we emphasized how vital it is to get a buyer to *come and see* your car. Buyers may be thin on the ground or there may be a lot of similar cars advertised on the day your ad, appears. Either way you cannot afford to miss out on any likely potential buyers!

Giving an indication of geographical location (the telephone exchange name may be enough by itself) prevents wasted calls from people too far away. A buyer may come a long distance however for an exceptionally rare car.

There is a limitless number of other possible things that can be added to your basic wording but, for a run of the mill mass produced car, they are mostly a waste of time and money. Put yourself always in the buyer's shoes to see whether the extra information you are considering adding is likely to be of much interest. Fundamentally all he wants to know is what car it is, how old, how much, and where it is. Your price alone is sufficient to give him a good indication of the condition. It is probably worth mentioning if a car happens to have had a new engine recently.

An exclusive car however, is a different matter. If it is not too old, the condition is good, and the appropriate market value is big, then it merits more descriptive wording. If you are shooting for big money, you have to use a big gun! A mean looking advertisement for this sort of car only brings along mean looking buyers! So do not be cheap about the wording.

In any wording you use, be positive. Trite negatives, like 'Don't look elsewhere' are a waste of money. A phrase of urgency, e.g. 'Must be seen' is useful. A well chosen adjective or a nicely turned phrase (provided it is truthful) can give your ad. that touch of class to which so many aspire but few attain. Some good adjectives and phrases which are indirectly descriptive (and therefore fall in the realm of matters

117

of opinion regarding the car) are: excellent: distinctive: Exceptional value: immaculate: in mint condition: outstanding example: must be the most magnificent of its type: superbly maintained. Precise descriptions, such as: original condition: unblemished: as new, and similar ones, must be avoided unless they are *strictly* accurate, to the letter. Otherwise you might find yourself in trouble for giving a false description. But any adjective must be used carefully.

Doubling up of adjectives tends to weaken the main one. The word 'real' in front of 'bargain' dilutes the force of that word rather than increasing it, for example. Either the car is a bargain or it is not. 'Real' can be described as a redundant adjective.

But if you are not good at thinking up colourful adjectives to glamorize your car, do not worry. It is a well known fact of advertising that the strictly descriptive advertisement pulls as well as or better in most instances than its gimmicky counterpart.

In describing a more exclusive car you can therefore be quite content with just giving *more* information. Give it neatly. A good introductory phrase such as 'fitted with' adds polish to a list of desirable extras which you may be including with the car. 'Finished in sage-green over smoke-grey' is a compact and compelling example of how to describe the colour.

Colour, though it may have no bearing on the utility of the car, seems to have considerable importance in attracting certain buyers. State if a colour is metallic. Mention the *interior* colour and state if is 'matching'. (Another word which helps to engender desire.)

Your name before the phone number is appealing, especially your christian name.

Only expensive extras are really worth mentioning, e.g. sunshine roof: power assisted brakes/steering: radio/tape deck (state if stereo, etc.): alloy wheels: special seats (e.g. reclining): undersealed: tinted glass: air conditioning.

Other points about your car which proclaim its desirability and exclusiveness may be well worth including if

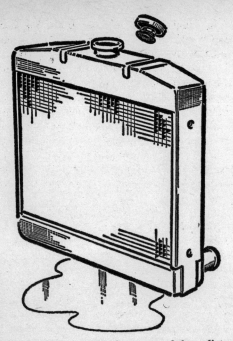

Fig. 19. Look for water leakage around the radiator, not
necessarily a big leak, a wet part in the matrix is enough.

they apply. Some good examples are: one owner: chauffeur
driven: director's car: lady director's personal car: complete
service history: the *recorded* mileage (unless it is unusually
high): month of manufacture (if it happens to be a late
month in the year): registration code letter (if it was one of
the first to have the new letter): any special tuning performance conversion to engine (give name of company
carrying out the work if well known). In the case of a his-
toric car it is important to say 'restored' or 'full engine rebuild' or whatever applies. You could mention some rally
successes when selling a racing sports car, or your own name
if you are a well known winner.

The reason that it has become the standard practice to

give the *recorded* mileage is to avoid any later argument over whether the mileage quoted was true. Theoretically you are safeguarded by the fact that you have only stated what the speedometer/odometer *recorded*, without including responsibility for its accuracy.

To save space there are a few common abbreviations. My advice is to avoid any except the most obvious ones, but to help you translate if you are looking for a car, there is a list of them in Chapter 8.

Among the popular daily media there are many who are in the habit of trying to persuade advertisers that they should have their ad. repeated with several consecutive day insertions to 'make sure'. Usually a discount or perhaps one 'free' repeat is offered, in order to tempt you. Frankly it's a lot of nonsense (apart from being a good money spinner for the media)! It is a very expensive way of telling a tiny proportion of new readers about your car. Indeed many bargain hunters wait for the last insertion before ringing up hoping you will by then be more desperate to sell!

Examples of Advertisements
Bare minimum ad. sufficient for a mass production model (placed in the Austin classification):

MAXI 1750 '74, £0,000, 043-689-1161 (Sussex), evenings 2240.

Slightly more generous ad, for a mass produced car which happens to be in particularly good order (put under Ford)

ESCORT 1300 XL '74, 4-door, white, 11,000 recorded miles: excellent: £0,000: 043-689-1161 (Sussex), evenings 2240.

For an exclusive car (positioned in the Triumph section):

STAG AUTOMATIC Dec. 1974 (N), finished in damson

with contrasting black trim, factory undersealed, luxuriously equipped with hard and soft tops, P.A.S., stereo radio/cassette player, tinted glass, managing director's personal transport from new, 12,000 recorded miles – outstanding example must be seen – £0,000 Christopher Sprake, 043-689-1161 (Sussex), evenings 2240.

Shop Window Post-cards

Surprisingly, although such a small number of people probably see such a car in a local shop window, they do get talked about within a local community and they often work! Therefore, if you are not in too much hurry to reach the widest possible market you could try locally first with an advertisement typed or hand printed onto a post-card. Your wording should follow the general principles outlined above and, to attract attention to *your* card, a good idea is to crayon the border in a bright colour. Red, psychologically, is likely to be the best colour.

8

Amusing Expressions, Common Jargon and Explanations of Abbreviations

Motor Trade expressions
The motor trade has long had a colourful repertoire of useful expressions. Some we include because you may come across them with bewilderment, others for their amusing nature! Those concerned with money we deal with first in order of value and the rest are in alphabetical order.

50p	a Wilson
£1	sheet
£5	fistful
£10	spot
£25	daughter
£50	pony
£75	three parts
£100	ton
£500	monkey
£1,000	grand

The 'bible'	Glass's Guide (see page 23)
The Bin	the bank
Bottler	car which will not sell
Bullet – has it got?	is it taxed?
Cack-hander	car with left hand drive
Clocked car	car with wound back speedo-meter/odometer

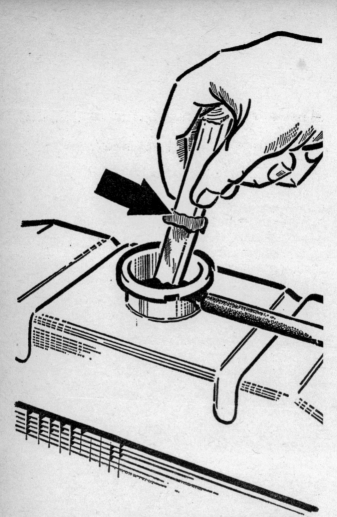

Fig. 20. Remove the radiator cap, or *instead*, the expansion tank cap if fitted; (not when the radiator is hot), then insert a piece of clean dry wood into the water and withdraw it. If the wood is covered with oil, there is an oil leakage into the cooling system, indicating at least a defective cylinder head gasket. A *trace* of oil is acceptable, but no more.

Death's bladders	dangerous tyres
Dog	bad car
Drive now – pay later	offer of hire purchase
Flyer	bouncing cheque
Four on the floor	floor manual gear change
Gas	petrol
Gleamer	clean or perfect car
Got'ch'a seats	reclining seats
Hole in the roof	sunshine roof
Hot window	heated rear window
Is it a runner?	does it go?
Jam jar	car
Jellybone	telephone
Jungle Juice	petrol
Kangaroo	Australian car
Kite	cheque
Lulu	clean or perfect car, same as 'gleamer'
Mickey Mouse	automatic transmission car
Mill	the engine
Mint	perfect condition
Nail	car ready for the scrap heap
Notes or rubber money?	will you pay by cash or by cheque
On the drip	buying by hire purchase
Over the hurdles	buying by hire purchase
Punter	prospective customer

Rat up a drain pipe (goes like a)	description of fast car
Ringer	stolen car
Slicks	tyres
Spin Bin	a Mini
Stand in price	equivalent total cash price paid by a trader for stock taken in in part exchange
Stitched up	the condition of having paid too much for a car
Stock	cars on sale by a trader
Ticket	road tax disc
Trip round the houses	demonstration run
Two skeletons joculating on a tin roof	description of a bad engine which clatters as it runs
William Bottle (Mr., going to consult)	referring to Glass's Guide
Wets	special tyres suited to racing on wet surfaces
Yank	American car.

Advertisement abbreviations

A H or A/H	air horns
A T or A/T	automatic transmission
B H P	brake horse power
B R G	British racing green
D/H or D H C	drop head coupé
E W or E/W	electric windows
F H C	fixed head coupé

FM/AM Radio	radio suitable to receive VHF (very high frequency) waves
F W D	front wheel drive
H P	horse power, or, hire purchase
H R W	heated rear window
H/S tops	hard and soft tops
L H D	left hand drive
L S D	limited slip differential
L W B	long wheel base
O/D	overdrive
O N O	or near offer
Onr	owner
O V N O	or very near offer
PB/radio	push button radio
P/B or P A B	power assisted brakes
P A S	power assisted steering
P/W or P A W	power assisted windows
PX or P/ex	part exchange
Q I spots	Quartz iodene spotlights
R/C L	reclining seats
R H D	right hand drive
R M	recorded mileage
S R	sunshine roof
S W B	short wheel base
V G C	very good condition
W/W or Wires	wire wheels.

LEARNING TO DRIVE IN PICTURES
by A. Tom Topper

The *first* book to really *attack* the difficulties simply and logically. The first quarter of this 208-page book – teaches absolute mastery of car control *to be* practised on open spaces or quiet, safe back streets. Step-by-step methods for achieving perfect three-point turns, reverses into openings and hill starts (the three major bugbears) are all taught BEFORE throwing you in the deep end of thick traffic.

Many have been frightened off learning to drive by appalling instruction and trying to learn things far out of their depth to begin with. A few awful frights and the whole project seems to become a hysterical nightmare. All this can be avoided with Tom Topper, the master teacher.

THE AUTHOR DIAGNOSES DANGER MET IN DRIVING
THE ESSENTIAL MASTER-DRIVING LIFE-SAVING POINTS are not glossed over and ignored – each is emphasized and explained, so that a child of 12 could understand.

Wonderful reviews appeared on publication and here are some extracts:

> *The Times:* 'Down-to-earth . . . practical . . . basic'
> *Daily Telegraph:* 'For those who are still struggling . . . good value'
> *Daily Mirror:* 'Clearer than many more expensive manuals'
> *The Sun:* 'Admirable . . . amazingly cheap . . . invaluable'
> *Daily Sketch:* 'Easiest to understand . . . excellent'
> *Woman's Own:* 'Very helpful . . . gives all the theory'

More publicity was accorded when the 2nd edition appeared by the *Daily Mail*, *Woman's Own* again and London *Evening News*, etc.

The enormous 1st edition of six figures was sold within months under our famous 'Test pass or money back guarantee'. We had none returned.

Uniform with this volume